Keys to the
Elementary
Classroom

THIRD EDITION

This edition of Keys to the Classroom is dedicated in memory of our co-author, Judy Stobbe, for dedicating her life to improving education for English Learners and to enriching the art of teaching.

Keys to the Elementary Classroom

THIRD EDITION

A **New Teacher's Guide** to the **First Month of School**

Carrol Moran
Judy Stobbe
Wendy Baron
Janette Miller
Ellen Moir

CORWIN PRESS
A SAGE Company

For information:

Corwin Press
A SAGE Company
2455 Teller Road
Thousand Oaks, California 91320
www.corwinpress.com

SAGE Ltd.
1 Oliver's Yard
55 City Road
London, EC1Y 1SP
United Kingdom

SAGE India Pvt. Ltd.
B 1/I 1 Mohan Cooperative
Industrial Area
Mathura Road, New Delhi 110 044
India

SAGE Asia-Pacific Pte. Ltd.
33 Pekin Street #02-01
Far East Square
Singapore 048763

Printed in the United States of America

Library of Congress Cataloging-in-Publication Data
Keys to the elementary classroom : a new teacher's guide to the first
month of school / Carrol Moran . . . [et al.]. — 3rd ed.
    p. cm.
English and Spanish.
Revised ed. of: Keys to the classroom, 2000.
Includes bibliographical references.
  ISBN 978-1-4129-6368-8 (cloth : acid-free paper) — ISBN
978-1-4129-6369-5 (pbk. : acid-free paper)
  1. Elementary school teaching—Handbooks, manuals, etc. 2. Education,
Elementary—Curricula--Handbooks, manuals, etc. 3. First year
Teachers—Handbooks, manuals, etc. I. Moran, Carrol. II. Title.

LB1555.K49 2009
372.1102—dc22

2008008417

This book is printed on acid-free paper.

08   09   10   11   10   9   8   7   6   5   4   3   2   1

Acquisition Editor: Carol Chambers Collins
Associate Editor: Desirée Enayati
Editorial Assistant: Brett Ory
Production Editor: Appingo Publishing Services
Cover Designer: Rose Storey
Graphic Designer: Karine Hovsepian

Contents

Acknowledgments

We would like to thank the loyal supporters and new teachers who have used this guide for the past twenty years. They showed us very clearly how crucial the first month is in setting the standards of interaction for the rest of the year.

We would also like to thank the new teacher mentors from the New Teacher Center who reviewed the last edition and gave us feedback on what worked and what might need to be changed or updated.

In addition, we would also like to thank our typists; our translator, Luz María S. Steves; and our graphic artist, Carrie Wilker, for the wonderful work they have done.

It is our hope in creating this guide that we can ease new teachers' entry into classroom teaching. We want to take the mystery out of the first month, and we have tried to spell out clearly the many keys used by experienced teachers to open the school year successfully.

Carrol Moran, Judy Stobbe, Wendy Baron,
Janette Miller, & Ellen Moir

PUBLISHER'S ACKNOWLEDGMENTS

Corwin Press would also like to thank the following reviewers:

Janet Crews, Instructional Coach
Clayton School District
Clayton, MO

Cathy Galland, Curriculum Director
Republic R-III School District
Republic, MO

Catherine Hernandez, Second-Grade Teacher
Detroit Public Schools
Detroit, MI

Greg Keith, Middle School Academic Coordinator
Department of Academic Affairs
Memphis, TN

Maureen Maloney, Second-Grade Teacher
Lusher Charter School
New Orleans, LA

Melanie Mares, Academic Coach
Lowndes Middle School
Valdosta, GA

David L. Sechler, Retired Middle School Principal
Dover, DE

About the Authors

Carrol Moran has worked in education for over thirty years. Her teaching experience encompasses preschool to graduate school, focusing on low-income students of diverse language backgrounds. She earned her BA from University of California, Santa Cruz; her Master's Degree from San Jose State University; and her PhD in Education, Language Literacy, and Culture, from Stanford University. She was a writer for Macmillan McGraw-Hill on materials for English Learners. She has published over twenty articles and books on education, including "Bilingual Education: Broadening Research Perspectives," published in *The Handbook of Research on Multicultural Education* and *A Balanced Approach to Literacy*, a resource document and introduction to K–3 literacy in teacher-education faculty programs. She is coauthor on "Rethinking English Language Instruction an Architectural Approach" in *English Learners: Reaching the Highest Level of English Literacy* (editor, Gilbert Garcia), and she is the editor of *Success by Design: The Work of the UC Santa Cruz Educational Partnership Center*. For the past twelve years, she has served as Executive Director of the Monterey Bay Educational Consortium and the UC Santa Cruz Educational Partnership Center.

Judy Stobbe is currently a classroom teacher and staff development specialist in a two-way bilingual immersion program specializing in emergent literacy, effective math instruction, second-language acquisition, and effective bilingual education. She has initiated a staff development model based on ongoing teacher collaboration that links authentic assessment to innovative classroom practices across an entire school. In her work as Staff Development Specialist, she has worked with a wide range of teachers—from preservice to the most experienced. Outside the classroom, she has written curriculum and articles for a variety of publications, including *Into English!: Kindergarten Teacher's Guide*, *The Bilingual Classroom*, for the DLM Early Childhood Program, *Access to Science: Activities and Strategies for Students Acquiring English Kindergarten–Grade 2*, and, coauthored with Carrol Moran,

"Strategies for Working with Overage Students," published in *The Power of Two Languages: Literacy and Biliteracy for Spanish-Speaking Students*.

Janette Miller has taught grades K–6, served as a reading specialist, evaluated new employees in Santa Cruz City Schools District, and supported new teachers through the Santa Cruz New Teacher Project. She has extensive training in classroom management, peer coaching, and evaluation. She has particularly enjoyed training novice and veteran teachers in classroom management techniques, direct teaching model, the reading/writing connection, and conceptual math strategies. Currently she is a Cotsen Family Foundation mentor working with veteran teachers to improve their practices.

Wendy Baron has taught grades K–6, served as a Title I Reading Specialist, supervised and instructed prospective teachers at the University of California, Santa Cruz, and for the past twenty years has worked directly with new teachers and principals, K–12. As associate director with the New Teacher Center at the University of California, Santa Cruz, Wendy oversees the Santa Cruz/Silicon Valley New Teacher Project, which supports over a thousand new teachers annually. She also consults with school districts throughout California and nationally on mentoring, teacher induction, and designing professional development for beginning teachers. Wendy has extensive experience in coaching, adult learning theory, group facilitation and professional development. She is a researcher and practitioner, and seeks continually to impact educational systems to support teacher development. Wendy is the author of several articles and book chapters and has produced numerous videos related to mentoring and new teacher development.

Ellen Moir is founder and executive director of the New Teacher Center at the University of California, Santa Cruz, which is committed to the development of an inspired, dedicated, and highly qualified teaching force by supporting new teachers as they enter the profession. For more than twenty years, she has pioneered innovative approaches to new teacher development, research on new teacher practice, and the design and administration of teacher induction programs. Ellen continues to work with the Santa Cruz/Silicon Valley New Teacher Project and is an advocate for new teachers across the country. Ellen has received national recognition for her work, including the Harold W. McGraw, Jr. 2005 Prize in Education and the 2003 Distinguished Teacher Educator Award from the California Council on Teacher Education. Ellen is the author of several articles and book chapters and has produced video series related to new teacher development. Her work has been supported by over twenty private foundations and donors, the National Science Foundation, and several state and federal agencies.

Introduction

Welcome to teaching! The future of our children is now in your hands. You are entering a complex and challenging profession. We believe you deserve as much help as possible to do an outstanding job. *Keys to the Elementary Classroom, Third Edition* will provide you, the new teacher, essential keys for a successful first year. This third edition of *Keys to the Elementary Classroom* incorporates the input of many new and veteran teachers, including a new Chapter 1, "A Guide to Planning and Creating the Environment," updated assessment materials, new English as a second language materials, and several new classroom activities.

Our revised textbook guides you in using your first month as a foundation for a successful year. Following are the elements used to create a rich learning environment:

- ◆ Build a sense of community to include all students
- ◆ Establish clear routines and procedures for your class
- ◆ Assess your students' strengths and needs
- ◆ Create an environment that fosters a love of learning

These elements are at the heart of a good beginning and are important to keep in mind, not only at the start of the school year but throughout it. *Keys to the Elementary Classroom*'s third edition offers greater detail and a more expanded format than the original text. Following are chapter highlights:

- ◆ Chapter 1, A Guide to Planning and Creating the Environment, offers an approach to long-term planning used in establishing the appropriate standards-based context for daily activities. Templates are included to help you think through approaches to each subject area. It also assists you in organizing your classroom and in providing your students with a stimulating learning environment. Also included are suggestions on classroom arrangement and instructional materials.
- ◆ Chapter 2, Assessments, assists in designing classroom-based assessments. Knowing your students' skills and abilities is crucial in providing them with appropriate instruction.
- ◆ Chapter 3, Routines and Procedures, suggests ways to establish both rhythm and structure to your days. Students feel more comfortable when they know what is expected. Clear, consistent routines and procedures eliminate most behavior problems. New teachers often need

the most help with this topic. By following the suggested practices, your classroom will run more smoothly.

♦ Chapter 4, The First Two Weeks of School . . . A Detailed Account guides you through the first weeks, day by day and minute by minute. This detailed account provides a daily structure, plus a timeline for introducing new routines, procedures, and activities. Greater detail to K–1 is provided here, with the assumption that those procedures will be incorporated into other grades. However, as a new teacher, you may wish to read the entire chapter before focusing on your specific grade level. This chapter is a treasure trove of thoughtful teaching, based on years of teacher experience.

♦ Chapter 5, Activities for the First Month, describes tried-and-true activities that can be used as the core of your program, or as a back-up plan. Student worksheets, copy-ready, are provided in English and Spanish. These can be included with planned activities or used as "easy assignment" for a substitute.

♦ Chapter 6, Fingerplays and Songs for Oral Language in English and Spanish, provides community building activities for language development and transitions for K–3 students.

♦ Chapter 7, Home and School Communication, suggests ways to develop relationships with students' families and provides a simple letter for adapting to English and Spanish.

♦ Chapter 8, Resources, offers many excellent books for the advancement of professional development.

Keys to the Elementary Classroom is certain to get you off to a good start. In addition to the suggestions and resources provided, we urge you to find an experienced teacher to serve as your mentor—either someone at your grade level, or one with an out-of-classroom position. Their support will be invaluable. New teachers should not attempt this complex job alone. *Find a mentor!*

PHASES OF TEACHING: THE UPS AND DOWNS OF A FIRST-YEAR TEACHER

Over the past two decades, the Santa Cruz New Teacher Project (SCNTP) worked with and conducted research on over two thousand new teachers. Their results will help you understand you are not alone, and that most new teachers have similar struggles during their first year. The project's research shows that new teachers experience five basic phases: (a) anticipation, (b) survival, (c) disillusionment, (d) rejuvenation, and (e) reflection. These are described below, including *new teacher quotes* for each phase. Descriptions are followed with suggestions for moving forward during each particular phase.

Anticipation

This phase begins during the student teaching portion of teacher preparation. New teachers enter with a tremendous commitment to make a difference, coupled with an idealistic view of how their goals will be accomplished: *I was elated to get the job, but terrified about going from the simulated experience of student teaching to that of the person in charge.* (This feeling of excitement often carries new teachers through the first few weeks of school.)

Suggestions: Check out as many classrooms as possible. Try to get organized in advance. Set up your classroom environment as soon as you obtain a copy of Keys to the Classroom.

Before starting your teaching assignment, visit a variety of classrooms. If already teaching, search out opportunities to visit other classrooms during recess or lunch for a *reality check*. Your visits will be more meaningful if you have specific questions in mind.

Survival

Your first month may be overwhelming. As a new teacher, you are constantly learning at a rapid pace. New teachers are instantly bombarded with many unanticipated problems and situations. *So little time, so much to learn: I feel like I'm constantly running. It's hard to focus on other aspects of my life.* (It is not uncommon for new teachers to spend up to seventy hours per week on schoolwork—with minimal time to reflect on the experience. Particularly overwhelming is the constant need to develop curriculum.)

Suggestions: Time to cut back, save your creative energy for the essentials. Seek out support for time management and organizational strategies.

When in the survival phase, decide where planning can be reduced. Can you borrow an established reading/math curriculum to avoid daily inventing? Or, is it possible to reduce the number of student groups? Reassess your plan now, admitting you are only human and cannot be creative about each curriculum aspect during this first year. Set time limits for planning. Take at least one day off each weekend. Borrow lessons from colleagues, when appropriate, and rely on prepackaged curriculum.

Disillusionment

New teachers enter this phase following six to eight weeks of nonstop work and stress of varied length and intensity. Low morale, extensive time commitment, the realization that things are not proceeding as smoothly as they wish—all these contribute to the disenchantment period. At this stage, new teachers begin questioning both their commitment and competence; many become ill. Also during this time, new teachers are confronted with family conferences, Back-to-School Night, and their first formal evaluation.

Classroom management may also become a major source of distress: *I thought I'd be focusing more on curriculum, less on classroom management and discipline. I'm stressed because I have some very problematic students who are low academically, and I think about them every second that my eyes are open.*

In this phase, new teachers express self-doubt, have lower self-esteem, face complaints from family and friends, and question their professional commitment. Managing this phase may be the toughest challenge they face as a new teacher.

Suggestions: Double-check your routines and procedures, pare down intricate planning, do something nice for yourself. Remember to breathe! Take care of yourself or you will become ill. Take time to sit on a rock, go for a walk, and listen to music. Working more does not mean life will be smoother. Reduce your level of complexity without decreasing your expectations for students.

This week, a basic math lesson from the book will be fine. Research keys for new activities to carry you through the next few days. Hints: get help from a mentor, borrow a lesson plan from another teacher, talk with fellow new teachers—they are experiencing the same thing. You are not alone. You will get through this!

Rejuvenation

This phase is characterized by a rise in new teachers' attitude toward teaching—a fresh sense of hopefulness starting usually in January, or following your first extended break. Breaks offer opportunities to relax, reflect, organize materials, and plan curriculum. Teachers acquire a new perspective, with a better understanding of the system, a more realistic acceptance of their teaching, coupled with a sense of accomplishment at having made it through the first, and most difficult, time of the school year. Although still months away, school year's ending becomes the proverbial light at the end of the tunnel. Now, teachers begin to feel more confident about their management skills: *I'm really excited about my story writing center, although my organization has at times been haphazard. Story writing has definitely revived my journals.*

This phase may last into spring, with many ups and downs along the way. Near the end of this time, new teachers worry if all can be accomplished prior to the end of school. Once more questioning their effectiveness as teachers, they wonder how their students will perform on tests: *I'm fearful of these big tests. Can I be fired if my kids do poorly? I don't know enough about them to be cognizant of what I haven't taught, and I'm sure it's a lot.*

Suggestions: Review long-term planning and year-end expectations. This is a good time to take another look at these plans, using more realistic expectations. It is also a good time to determine what is expected for year-end exams, so students can be prepared in advance. Discuss your school's expectations for end-of-the-year closing with a mentor, resource teacher, or principal. This helps to spread out wrap-up activities over several months, without being caught off guard during the last month.

Reflection

This phase occurs during the last six weeks of school and can be an invigorating time for first-year teachers. Reflecting back, they can highlight successful events, and review changes to be made the following year in management, curriculum, and teaching strategies. The end is in sight. You've almost made it! More importantly, a vision for your second year emerges—a new phase of anticipation: *Next year, I'd like to start letter puppets earlier, so the kids can be introduced to more letters.*

Suggestions: Take notes on your reflections.

Review what worked and what did not. Make notes in your plan book to assist in planning the following year. You might think you will never forget this experience, but by the end of summer vacation, all will be a blur. Save yourself from repeating the same mistakes; benefit from new insights to create better lessons. Write it down!

We hope our research helps you realize that your experiences during this first year are normal phases of entering a complex, intense profession—one that cannot be mastered during any first year. Give yourself a break. Rely on *Keys to the Classroom* to get you started. When mistakes occur, remember: Be as kind to yourself as with any student in your classroom. Just like your students, you are doing the best you can!

Have a good first year!

A Guide to Planning and Creating the Environment

Good planning is the key to a successful first month of school. It builds confidence and enables your lessons to run smoothly and students to become engaged in the curriculum. Planning your lessons in detail during the first few weeks will help you to anticipate and prepare for problems in advance.

This chapter will provide a variety of planning strategies and tools for annual, midrange, daily, and weekly planning including sample daily calendars and schedules. It includes transitions from one task to another and various samples of daily and weekly activities. It also includes a section on planning focused on the needs of English learners.

This chapter also contains ideas to organize your classroom, room arrangements including centers for K–2 classrooms, lists of supplies, environment checklists, suggestions for first-day preparation including how to prepare class lists and bus and name tags. The chapter also provides you with a list of essential knowledge with which your should familiarize yourself prior to school starting regarding academics, equipment and machinery, school personnel, school procedures, and supplies.

ANNUAL PLANNING

The task of planning may seem overwhelming. To make it easier, first obtain copies of curriculum guides, frameworks, and content standards. Review any pacing guides that have already been developed for your grade level. Locate copies of texts, reading materials, and other relevant materials for your school and grade level. A good source for this information would be a veteran teacher or your principal. Become familiar with the big picture. Realize that throughout the year, you will make decisions concerning what to teach and the *length of time* students should be engaged in a particular unit. If possible meet with the other teachers at your grade level to collaborate on long-range planning.

◆ Review the Language Arts and Math Content Standards (content standards are published by State DOEs. California standards are available at: http://www.cde.ca.gov/be/st/ss/).

◆ Review curriculum guides, frameworks, texts, and literature associated with each content area, and compile a list or map of the specific subject matter and assessments. You will need both a calendar and a matrix to map out the year. You can do this with pencil and paper or on the computer. An Excel spreadsheet or simple Word table will work well for the creation of the matrix. Across the top list the months of the year. Down the left side list the subject areas to be covered.

Figure 1.1   Annual Plan

	Month			
Subject	**September**	**October**	**November**	**(Continue December through June)**
Reading	Assessments Comprehension Fluency	Summarizing Retelling	Plot analysis	
Math	Assessments Skills Problem solving	Chapters 1–4 Multiplication tables Logic problems	Chapters 5–9 Solving word problems	
Social Studies	The American Revolution	Development of constitutions Separation of powers	Early U.S. history Bill of Rights	

Use the above matrix and an Excel spreadsheet to map out the year to ensure coverage of any texts, materials, standards, and content required during the year. This rough sketch will be revised as you become familiar with your students' knowledge, skills, interests, and needs. Notice links between subject areas, and develop integrated, thematic units of study. Use the matrix for Back-to-School Night to inform family members of your year-long plan.

K–6: Lesson Plan Book

Obtain a copy of both the school and district master schedules. You may use a ready-made plan book or create your own on the computer. To create your own planner use a table that has the days of the week across the top and the time blocks with bell schedules down the side. Enter important dates in your plan book first in a monthly calendar to put the important dates and events for each month for quick review (i.e., Back-to-School Night, report cards, parent conferences, standardized testing dates, staff development days, special holidays, and school and district events). Then create a weekly planner with the dates and special events of the week and include your school's bell schedule, library time, restructured days, and mandated time for specific subjects. Plan carefully so your daily schedule will remain constant throughout the year.

Set up your plan book with dates for the year (look at a school calendar and put the starting and ending dates of the weeks of school at the top of the pages in your plan book and list all holidays). At the first teachers' meeting, you will probably receive various other important dates to remember. If you have your plan book set up, you can immediately transfer those important dates and responsibilities into your book so you don't forget them. The following are some examples:

- Yard duty for each week (this is important—put this right next to the date at the top of the page in red ink)
- Back-to-School Night
- Parent conferences
- Vacation days
- Staff development training
- Vision and hearing screenings
- Special events
- Testing schedule
- Report card deadlines
- Release time

Having the schedule set up ahead of time will relieve you of trying to find that calendar of events in your piles of papers. This is a good habit to get into: Every time you receive a piece of paper in your box with an important date, you have a place to write it down where you will remember to look at it!

When you set up your plan book, leave a space or column for a things to do and places to go list. List your major preparation here. Also list meeting times and places so you don't forget them.

MIDRANGE PLANNING: GETTING TO KNOW YOUR STUDENTS AND COMMUNITY

Once you have a sense of the school year, it's time to think in terms of units of study. We suggest the beginning-of-the-year theme, *Getting to Know You*, which will be used as an example of how to develop integrated, thematic unit planning. Start with these questions:

♦ *Who are my students, and what do they bring?* Surveying students' interests and backgrounds and assessing their skills regularly will enable you to match your instruction to your students. Use your knowledge of their experiences, families, and community to create relevant lessons. Phone each family or visit them at home. Familiarize yourself with the school community.

Review all the information available to you from former teachers and cumulative records. Create a profile sheet (see sample below) with the name of students down the left and the assessment information you will be using across the top. These assessments include language status, ability in English, ability in reading, math, and special categories for students (migrant, special education, speech, gifted, etc.). This class profile list will help you in determining groups for differentiated instruction.

Figure 1.2   Sample Class Profile Sheet

Teacher: Mrs. Campos
Grade: Third

Student Names	Primary Language	ELD Level	Reading Fluency	Reading Comp.	Math Level	Special Designation	Bus #	Writing	GATE	Migrant
1. Maria Aguilar	Spanish	3	50	75	5		92	Med	X	X
2. Ye Keo	Cambodian	2	30	45	4	Speech	75	Low		
3. Hanja Kim	Korean	FEP	20	75	3.5	Special Ed	Walk	High		
4. Joe Smith	English	EO	60	80	4	ADD				
5. Sarah Zaad	English	EO	70	90	6				X	

◆ *What do I want them to know and become able to accomplish?* Knowing your subject matter and having short- and long-term learning goals will help you clarify what to focus your instruction on. Consider which assessments enable you to learn what your students know and are able to accomplish. These should guide the planning, selection, and sequencing of activities and assist in making adjustments to your students' individual needs. Review standards and required texts to determine what skills and content you will be covering during the year.

◆ *How will I move them forward?* You will be most successful if you choose a variety of instructional strategies to match what students will learn. Promote critical thinking and problem solving within each lesson. Use resources and materials that all students can use and understand, and incorporate learning materials to reflect the linguistic and academic diversity of your classroom. Provide experiences that promote interaction, autonomy, and choice. Teach procedures for each activity within the lesson. Model expected behaviors and provide examples of the quality of work expected of the students.

◆ *How will I know what they have learned?* Use multiple measures for assessing student learning. For example, it is possible to assess students' understanding of concepts through story retellings, written reports, projects, oral presentations, timed tests, worksheets, anecdotal records, written stories, visual displays, and physical demonstration of skills. Involve students in developing criteria (or a grading system) for completed products by assessing and reflecting on their work and by setting personal learning goals based on their assessments. Use assessment results to guide instruction and to improve your assignments. Involve parents and guardians as assessment partners. Communicate often about their child's progress (see Chapter 2, Assessments).

See Tables 1.1 through 1.3 for specific examples of planning tools and activities. To recap the elements basic to midrange planning:

◆ Know the content and subject matter. Determine what students know and are interested in learning.
◆ Use standards to develop goals for student learning.
◆ Assess students to create baseline assessment data in language, literacy, math, etc.
◆ List possible activities and assessment strategies to develop lessons.

DAILY AND WEEKLY PLANNING

Table 1.1   Theme: Getting to Know You; Possible Activities and Assessments—Intermediate

Build a Community of Learners	*Implement Classroom Procedures and Routines*	*Include Transition Activities*	*Establish Standards for Behavior: Rules and Consequences*	*Assessments*
Paired Interviews Name Games Find Someone Who . . . Graffiti Boards Me Pictures Shields Partner Drawings Name Scramble 2	**Procedures Needed** Getting quiet Entering and leaving classroom Equipment checkout Jobs and monitors Snack time and lunch Independent work Group work Outside, PE behavior Homework "Transition activities"	**Transition Activities** (following recess): Sustained silent reading Journals Sentence corrections Read-aloud time Math warm-ups	**Rules** Please/Please Don't Develop four class rules from Please/Please Don't Illustrate rules—individual books Group skits to show examples of rules **Consequences** *Positive*: Group points for being at task, being ready *Negative*: 1. Give warning 2. Time out in class 3. Recess, other class 4. Call home, meet with parents **Other** Appreciation words Positive adjectives Conflict resolution Problem-solving skits	**Literacy** Read aloud vignettes from *House on Mango Street* Morning Messages Names: scramble, origins, sort Think-Alouds—personal stories Personal Stories—writing process **Math** Graphing unit (bar, picture, line) Letters in name Month of birthday Eye color Favorite ice cream (out of three flavors) Favorite TV show Travel to school Like to be when grown up **Reading** Oral reading and comprehension assessment What I Think About Reading **Writing** Wiggly Line Personal stories What I Think About Writing **Math** Computation Problem solving What I Think About Math **Other** Attitude Line-Up Introducing How I Feel

Table 1.2   Theme: Getting to Know You; First Week of School—Grades 4 to 6

	Monday	*Tuesday*	*Wednesday*	*Thursday*	*Friday*
8:30–10:00	Welcome Attention signal Introductions Name Scramble 2 Letters Getting ready for recess	Opening Sentence corrections Literacy—*Names*	Opening Journals Literacy—*House on Mango Street* Prewrite "Memorable Moment" Early finishers: SSR, journal, worksheet	Opening Sentence corrections Literacy—*Laughter* Oral paragraphs First drafts	Opening Journals Literacy—*Rice Sandwich* Finish first drafts
10:00–10:15	Recess	Recess— Yard duty	Recess	Recess— Yard duty	Recess
10:15–11:30	Math warm-up Math-graphing KWL Please/Please Don't Before-lunch procedures	Math warm-up Math—bar graph, "Careers" Please/Please Don't, Part 2	Math warm-up Math—Students create bar graphs Names games, initial adjectives	SSR Math warm-up Math—Line graph Partner surveys	Math warm-up Math—Circle graph "What I Think About Math" survey
11:30–12:15	Lunch	Lunch	Lunch	Lunch	Lunch
12:15–1:30	Read aloud Know Your Classmates	Read aloud Partner drawings	Read aloud Shields	Read aloud Finish Shields	Read aloud What Makes a Good Listener?
1:30–2:30	Homework Jobs PE (knots) Closure and dismissal	Homework Jobs PE (cooperative relays) Closure and dismissal	Homework Jobs PE (running laps) Closure and dismissal	Homework Jobs PE (stretching) Closure and dismissal	Homework Jobs PE Closure and dismissal

Table 1.3   Theme: Getting to Know You; Second Week of School—Grades 4 to 6

	Monday	**Tuesday**	**Wednesday**	**Thursday**	**Friday**
8:30–10:00	Opening Sentence corrections Literacy—*And Some More* Feedback on stories	Opening Journals Literacy—*First Job*	Opening Sentence corrections Literacy—*Core literature*	Opening Journals Literacy—*Core literature*	Opening Sentence corrections Literacy—*Core literature* "What I Think About Writing"
10:00–10:15	Recess	Recess—Yard duty	Recess	Recess—Yard duty	Recess
10:15–11:30	SSR Math warm-up Math—Begin project "What I Think About Reading" survey	SSR Writer's Workshop—peer edit Math warm-up Math—Develop rubric	SSR Writer's Workshop—final draft Math warm-up Math—Finish graphs	SSR Writer's Workshop—Illustrations Math warm-up Math—Self-assess and trade graphs	SSR Writer's Workshop—Cover, title page, About the Author Math warm-up Math—KWL, pretest
11:30–12:15	Lunch	Lunch	Lunch	Lunch	Lunch
12:15–1:30	Read aloud I Messages	Read aloud Appreciation words Graffiti boards	Read aloud Problem-solving skits	Read aloud Emotions	Read aloud Group definition of cooperation and cooperative triangles
1:30–2:30	Homework PE Jobs Closure and dismissal	Homework—Line graphs PE Jobs Closure and dismissal	Homework PE Jobs Closure and dismissal	Homework PE Jobs Closure and dismissal	Homework PE Jobs Closure and dismissal

Daily Calendar

In your plan book create a daily calendar showing your bell schedule for recesses and lunch. Include all known times: library, PE, music, and so forth. If your school has special activities during the week or year, list those in your plan book right away.

Subject Schedule

Determine the schedule for individual subjects, combinations of subjects, or themes. Consider a possible theme time integrating social studies, language arts, music, and art during the day. Determine how your schedule fits with possible team interaction. If you have English learners in your classroom, determine how they will get systematic English language instruction at the appropriate level daily in a small group. Determine when you will do frontloading for new vocabulary or structures in the text and how you will shelter content for English learners.

Transition Activities

Brainstorm transition and routine activities occurring after each recess. Some examples are journals, math warm-ups, sentence corrections, sustained silent reading (SSR), and read-alouds. Decide about placement in your daily schedule. If you routinely have a transition activity after each recess, it will allow you time to meet with students as needed, to assess them individually, or to complete preparation for the next activity. These routines should be explicitly taught during the first month so students may practice their expected behavior.

Daily and Weekly Activities

Consider other daily and weekly activities, such as morning message, calendar, daily agenda, jobs, homework assignments, current events, quizzes, tests, and class meetings. Enter these in your plan book.

You now have a basic daily and weekly schedule. While scheduling your midrange planning, you can add the sequence of activities for each unit and series of lessons.

Certain lessons require more details than others. Consider adding a basic plan structure to your plan book. Another notebook may include more specific plans: for instance, an introduction to the lesson or set, instruction, guided practice, independent practice, and closure. A detailed outline for routine procedures is necessary only for initial teaching, to assist you in planning the routine's procedures, modeling, and practice.

Careful planning does not imply that these are etched in stone. Your students' backgrounds, interests, and needs will drive your instruction. Plans can serve as a road map, but remember: The route may be changed whenever needed!

Planning for English Learners

You must learn the capabilities of both the English and the content of each of your English learners. There are required assessments for English language—learn what those are in your state and district. Find out from your students' record at what level they have been assessed, and use that as a starting point to begin to determine what language needs students have. When you assess students in subject areas, keep in mind that their language skills may hide greater abilities in reading or math. To determine the subject area skills you may need to bring in someone who speaks the language of the English learner. Give simple assessments of mathematics and reading that will allow you to determine if a learner has sound symbol and numeric relationships. You will need to plan for three strands of addressing language needs: (1) *Systematic English language development*. Students should receive twenty to thirty minutes of instruction daily in English at an appropriate level. If the student is a beginner in English s/he needs to be grouped with other beginners for this systematic approach to English. This may require working across classrooms to provide the small group instruction needed; (2) *Intentional teaching of needed vocabulary and structures* of lessons; (3) *Sheltered strategies to clue in English learners* to understanding and participating in content area instruction. These three strands on English instruction all require planning on a weekly basis.

Systematic English Language Development

There are a variety of programs that provide a systematic approach to teaching English. Systematic English language development moves students through the developmental levels of learning English from simple beginning structures and vocabulary to more complex language. It ensures that students learn all of the basic language they will need to function in school. This should be done in small groups with other students at the same level of learning English and may be organized across grade level teams or across larger school groups depending on the numbers of English learners in the school.

Intentional Teaching of Language Structures and Functions and Vocabulary

Look at each of the units you will be covering during the first month of school. Think about what the vocabulary is that students will need to use in each of these units. Plan out in advance how you will teach that vocabulary. Create charts for the walls that students can refer to with pictures or definitions to help them remember the key vocabulary. Plan to create mind maps with your students or charts with the basic concept in the middle and webs that move from students' prior knowledge to the new vocabulary related to things students might already know.

Consider the ways in which students will need to use the language (functions) that they will need in the lessons. Will students be asked to describe something? If so, they will need to learn that adjectives in English usually precede the noun they are describing. Will you be asking students to introduce someone? If so, they will need to learn language structures used in introductions such as, "I would like to introduce you to. . .," "This is Maya. Maya is. . .," or "I want you to meet Khanvhi." If you are asking students to read word problems in mathematics, you will need to analyze those problems to be able to teach the structures the language students will need, not only to read those problems but also to answer the problems. For example: "If Joe has two apples and Mary gives him three apples, how many apples will Joe have?" In this problem your students will need to be able to use the "If. . .then" structures as well as the conjugations of the verb "to have." To answer the problem they will also need to use the future or conditional tense of "will."

Teaching language requires advanced planning not only of the content and vocabulary but also an analysis and planning of how those language structures will be taught and reinforced. There will be a need to pre-teach the structures for students to carry out those functions. Pre-teaching can be through role play, providing cloze sentences, "If he does ___, then ___ will happen." Whatever the lesson expectation, teach the language needed to meet that expectation. For example, your students need to write an essay on an animal. Consider the language they will need to describe the habitat, food, and functioning of an animal. Then teach the structures they will need to write the essay. Create charts for the walls, or individual help worksheets or booklets for English learners to refer to in scaffolding the lesson. For every lesson in each subject area you will need to plan ahead to analyze the text and lesson expectations to support your English learners in gaining access to the text.

Sheltered Strategies

Whatever the content you are teaching there are a number of strategies you can use to shelter a lesson, making it more understandable for English learning. Some strategies include using pictures, gestures, voice intonation, repetition, and writing key words on the board next to familiar words or pictures. You can start lessons with a mind map (putting the topic in the middle and mapping related ideas around the outside connected with lines to the main concept) that allows students to familiarize themselves with a topic and connect to prior knowledge. Creating hands-on experiences, allowing students to work together in pairs using cooperative strategies including specific roles in a group, etc., will give English learners more opportunities to participate. Graphic organizers, maps, and charts can help students organize information in a way that will help them learn the connections and the vocabulary. When you are planning your lesson try each week to come up with a couple of sheltered strategies that will help you get content across to your students, and write them into your planning guide for the week.

CREATING THE CLASSROOM ENVIRONMENT

A very important part of planning is organizing the environment for success. Organize your classroom in a way that allows for a variety of learning styles and situations and that keeps materials organized and accessible to students. You will want to think through how you will introduce your students to the room organization and train them to keep it clean and organized by putting things back in their proper place after an activity. Clearly coding the classroom will help keep it organized.

Room Arrangement

Environment plays a critical role in the classroom. How you set up your room affects the learning that will take place. Before students arrive, organize your room with an eye toward flexibility in the future.

Following are suggestions for activity areas. If space, furniture, and equipment do not allow setting these up as separate areas, you might rethink the storage of equipment and supplies so an area can be used for more than one center (i.e., an art center might be used as a teacher-directed lesson space if that center is not used during the time block for group instruction).

- Sufficient space for whole-group meetings on the floor (rug area) near a bulletin board—or within easy viewing of a chart stand when writing together
- Table large enough to work with groups or for teacher-directed small groups (two tables required if an aide assists with small groups)
- Art center with supply storage that can be easily accessed by students; if your center includes a table and easels, it can be maintained more easily if located near the sink
- Listening center for two to four students at a small table or on the floor; center should be equipped with tape recorder, two to four sets of earphones, and a jack for hooking earphones to the tape recorder
- Writing center with paper, pens, pencils, crayons, and markers stored in a clearly organized manner
- Center areas where two to four students can do independent study activities (e.g., small tables, individual desks, counter space, or floor areas)
- Library corner with thematic and current-interest books displayed so students may see their covers, plus additional space for a growing collection of student-authored books; also needed: inviting reading space with a comfortable chair, lamp, pillows, and so on (Note: On the first day, *do not* overstock the library. Allow the collection to grow as you read and write books together.)
- Observation and science area for objects your students bring to share for a particular theme (e.g., shells displayed for a sea life theme or objects with scents displayed for a five-senses theme)

- Dramatic-play area containing dolls, telephone, dishes, playhouse furniture, plastic food items, and so on; as different themes are studied during the year, this area can be converted to a museum, post office, grocery store, or doctor's office
- Construction area for blocks, LEGO®, or other manipulatives
- Computer center

Flexible use of space requires your students to understand *when* it is appropriate to be in a certain area or center. Prepare several Stop signs or Open–Closed two-sided signs that can be hung up when a particular center is not available. It is not necessary for each area to be up and running the first day. Area planning allows you to enrich your classroom with materials without rearranging furniture to gain additional space. Train students on how to use each center before allowing independent use. Such training should be a large part of your first month's instruction. Set up centers that are most critical to your instructional goals.

Seating (Dependent on Your Preference)

- Kindergartners need cubbies rather than assigned seating. On the first day, it is not necessary to label cubbies with students' names. During the following few days, they may choose their particular cubby. Having students decorate name cards for their cubbies is a good small-group lesson.
- First and second graders use tables or desks. If tables are used, students need cubbies for storing schoolwork, backpacks, and lunch boxes. First and second graders usually have assigned seats for part of the day, but this arrangement allows for seats to be used in various ways during the day (i.e., reading groups or centers).
- Third- to sixth-grade students may only use desks. Varied seating arrangements can be used, but we recommend that desks be grouped in fours or sixes to encourage cooperation. The first-day seating arrangement can be arbitrary, in alphabetical order, or by student choice. As you become familiar with students' behaviors and abilities, you can work together on making changes.

Organization of Supplies

Environment means more than furniture arrangement. Review your materials storage: crayons, glue, scissors, pencils, paper; also games, puzzles, blocks, books, manipulative materials, and so on.

Color code and symbol code general supplies so students can become independent when cleaning up. Store supplies in movable tubs or boxes labeled with the same color as the table or work area. Storage area for supplies should be labeled with the same color or shape. Example: If general supplies are needed in five areas, label each with a piece of laminated construction paper cut in these shapes: orange rectangle, red circle, green triangle, yellow square, blue oval.

Then, label five supply tubs (containing pencils, crayons, scissors, and glue or paste) with corresponding shapes. Last, label the area to return supplies with those same five shapes. Now, students can easily find and return supplies as needed. Other items used by students on a regular basis such as puzzles, math manipulatives, games, LEGO® blocks, and so on, can be stored consistently on shelves labeled with their names.

Environment Checklist

- ◆ Start with a few fiction and nonfiction books, remember to look for books that appeal to the range of students in your class (female and male characters of diverse backgrounds on a variety of topics), then add to your collection during the coming weeks. Younger children return to familiar books, and they read with greater concentration. Add to your collection of read-aloud books.
- ◆ Establish an inviting library corner. Students should have access to cassette tapes or CDs that accompany books. Auditory accompaniment will allow students to benefit from books that exceed their independent reading level.
- ◆ Have reading material other than books available (magazines, catalogs, and cards). Also make videos and CDs available.
- ◆ Include creative materials for students to express their own personal interpretations in project form.
- ◆ Make opportunities and materials available for students to conduct research and experiments.
- ◆ Allocate spaces for oral activities like Readers' Theater, choral speaking, and play acting that will not interfere with silent reading and listening activities.
- ◆ Provide blank cassette tapes for students to record or listen to their story readings, or both.
- ◆ Establish quiet corners for students to write, read, dream, and think. Hang bulletin boards to display students' work, allow for learning and interaction; support what is taught.
- ◆ Space should be neatly organized and designed for easy maintenance by the class community.
- ◆ The classroom should provide opportunities for students to choose from several activities and places or ways to work.

PREPARATION PRIOR TO THE FIRST DAY

Prepare the following before students arrive:

K–6 Class List

This includes all students' addresses, bus routes and stops, and telephone numbers. New students should be added to the list immediately. Refer to a map or take a tour of your attendance area to become familiar with neighborhoods and bus stops. Obtain this information from your school secretary or a veteran teacher, or ask them to be your tour guide (or both). Start by organizing your list in alphabetical order by *first name*. The school's list is prepared by *last* name. As you will be concentrating on learning students' first names, use of the school's list will slow you down. Also, students' given names are not necessarily what they use; for instance, if Maria Guadalupe is called Lupita, you'll become confused. Creating your own list is worth the effort.

A computer database is an efficient way to create a class list. Many types of integrated software are available: *AppleWorks*, *Microsoft Office*, *Microsoft Works*, and so on. This way, making changes and correcting errors becomes easier. Also, the database can be used to create labels for a substitute, field trips, bus transportation name tags, and so on.

K–6 Bus Tags and Bus List

Carefully research how your students will get home. Know their bus routes and stops, who will be picked up and by whom, and who will walk home and with whom. For younger students, this information is critical—you do not want to lose a student! Ask how to obtain this information from the school secretary or a veteran teacher at your grade level, then:

- ♦ Create a master bus list (in alphabetical order by first name) to be kept on a clipboard and carried with you to the bus lines.
- ♦ Prepare a *How We Get Home* graph, matching students to their respective buses. Post as a wall display for reference at dismissal time. (Creating this graph with students on the first day is a good opening-day, whole-group activity.)
- ♦ Prepare individual bus tags with students' first and last names, home address, phone number (optional), and bus route and stop. (If using a database, use the *print merge* option for address labels that include this information. Printed address labels equate to instant, easy-to-stick-on bus tags that may be prepared daily and reflect any class changes.)
- ♦ Depending on students' ages and their bus drivers' needs, some students wear bus tags for the first two weeks. Younger children need tags longer than older students. Bus drivers carry an enormous responsibility in making sure that students arrive home safely. Ask what is required of you so their jobs can run more smoothly.
- ♦ Decide if students should return their bus tags daily. If so, laminate the tags, and they can become lasting necklaces. Often, there are several students who do not return theirs and require new tags. Decide which is best: a master tag that can be copied onto address labels, printing new tags each time for all students, OR making new tags for those few students when needed. Decide on a time and procedure for figuring out who needs new tags. Remember to plan a time to make new tags each day.

K–6 Name Tags for Permanent Seats

Name tags can be prepared prior to the first day, or you might have students create name cards for their own permanent seats. One first-days goal is to build a sense of community and inclusion. Creating a climate where community members are known by name is an important part of this goal. The more ways that students can create their own communities, including working together on individual name cards, the better.

K–2 Name Tags

Wearable name tags must be prepared for each student. During the first day, one of your most important tasks will be to learn their names. The more visual information available, the faster names can be learned. Some schools have a high transiency rate, meaning that the list you receive before the first day may be inaccurate. Ask a veteran teacher or school secretary if this might occur at your site. If so, choose a tag style that can easily be changed or discarded.

Name tags can represent the special shape or character of your first theme. Create these from sturdy paper, laminated for use over several days. Attach roving or string to make necklaces—or you may purchase plastic holders affixed with a pin, clip, or string. These are inexpensive and available at office supply stores. Write names on the cards, add a sticker, and then slip each one into a plastic holder. These tags will survive the school year, can be available for a substitute's use, and are easily changed when a student leaves or arrives. When forming temporary groups for first-week activities, color code the name tags using different colors of roving or varied stickers. Place students with the same color roving or sticker into the same group. Collect name tags at day's end; replace with a bus tag, if appropriate.

In K–1, students might read the names each day as a whole group. One of the first things students learn to read are each other's names. Making this a routine provides many opportunities for teaching phonics in context.

K–6: Calendar. The classroom calendar should be up and ready to go. This calendar and its related activities constitute a routine you want to establish. It is relatively easy to get together and can be a ten- to twenty-minute activity done every day. See the section on the calendar routine in Chapter 3 for how to set one up.

K–2: Pre-Selected Read-Alouds. These should be short, with good illustrations and predictable, repetitive text. Having these pre-selected and within easy reach of the whole-group area will help with those moments that need to be filled. See the section on read-alouds in Chapter 8 for a bibliography.

3–6: Preselected Read-Alouds. Books that you really enjoy and that will capture the interest of your students make reading aloud an enjoyable part of the day.

K–2: Written List of Fingerplays and Songs. You should memorize and be ready with a repertoire of at least ten songs and fingerplays. See Chapter 6 for some easy ones. Student attention is more easily and gently gained through chanting and singing than through overt phrases, such as, "I need your attention." If you start a chant, soon all the students will join in.

K–6: File Folder for Each Student. Write each student's name on a file folder, and alphabetize the folders by first names. Have the files easily accessible in an open box or tub. Keep extra folders on hand for new arrivals. Having your folders ready will enable you to quickly file those beginning-of-the-year activities that you want to save (e.g., self-portraits, writing samples, teacher observations, parent notes).

K–6: Homework Tub or System. Set up a tub where students put their homework, notes from home, permission and other forms, and the like. Keep this in a consistent place near the door.

1–6: Individual Work Folders. Make each student a construction-paper folder labeled with his or her name. All daily work can be corrected or checked and filed. These folders should be kept in a central location, not in individual student desks. All work can be compiled and sent home on Friday or Monday to be reviewed and signed by parents. This provides one night a week of homework and the opportunity for parents to see their children's progress over a week's time.

K–6: Bulletin Boards. Create a learning environment that is interesting, inviting, and comfortable. Bulletin boards should reflect the atmosphere you want to have in your classroom.

- Leave at least one blank board for the display of an initial classroom project.
- Plan a welcome-type bulletin board (e.g., Famous Fourth Graders: put up pictures, names, interview information).
- Use your bulletin boards to tie into the beginning-of-the-year themes.

Many districts have teacher centers where you can use a die-cut machine to cut the letters that you need for bulletin boards. Teacher supply stores also may have prepackaged commercial bulletin boards. But to obtain maximum advantage from bulletin boards, you should involve students in the design, layout, and especially in the content.

Basics to Know About Your Classroom

Be sure you know how to find:

- Classroom keys, cabinet keys
- Classroom light switch
- Classroom heat control
- Intercom

Academics

- Cumulative records
- Diagnostic and placement tests
- Grade book
- Grade-level and subject expectations
- Library books, texts, workbooks
- Plan book
- Profiles, individual records

(Continued)

(Continued)

- Report cards
- Science and math manipulatives

- Standardized test results
- Student and home information

Equipment and Machinery

- Computers, flash drives, printer, paper, LCD projectors
- Cookware, stove
- Desks, chairs, tables
- Easels, chalkboards
- Electrical outlets
- Projectors, screen, extension cords

- Films, videos
- Laminator
- Dry-erase markers, whiteboard
- Pencil sharpener
- Photocopier, photocopier key
- Tape recorder
- Video and audio equipment

Personnel (Name, Schedule, Location)

- Paraprofessionals
- Cafeteria staff
- Custodians
- Fellow teachers

- GATE (Gifted and Talented Education) staff
- Nurse
- Secretary, office personnel
- Special education staff

Procedures

- Abuse and neglect reporting
- Bus rules and procedures
- Cafeteria rules
- Evacuation of building
- Field trips
- Fire, earthquake, or disaster plan
- Fire extinguisher
- Library and hall passes
- Location of all schedules
- Lunch money, tickets, charges

- Petty cash
- Phone procedures
- Playground rules
- Power outage
- Roll sheet
- Seating chart
- Student or staff illness
- Substitutes: number, plans
- Supply and purchase orders
- Weekly bulletin

Supplies

- Art supplies
- Chalk, chalkboard erasers
- Cleaning supplies: broom, dustpan, sponge, soap
- Clipboards
- Crayons
- Envelopes
- File folders
- First-aid kit
- Hole punch
- Tissues
- Label-making gun and tape
- PE equipment: whistle, stopwatch

- Paper: butcher, construction, scratch, writing, tagboard
- Paper clips
- Paper towels
- Paste, glue
- Pencils, erasers, pens
- Pins
- Post-it® notes
- Rubber bands
- Rulers
- Scissors
- Staplers, staples
- Stickers
- Tape: transparent, masking

2

Assessments

The chapter provides an overview of assessments to use as well as strategies to get to know your students and simple pre-assessment forms to gain information about your students' skill levels. These baseline assessments include quick reading assessments, writing rubrics, and quick math assessments, as well as student self-assessments of interests and learning styles.

ASSESSMENT OVERVIEW

There are three main types of assessment: pre-assessment (before learning), formative assessment (during learning), and summative assessment (after learning). This chapter will focus on pre-assessments to help you get baseline information on your students. The purpose of pre-assessment is to find out who the students are outside of school, individual learning styles and interests, study skills and current academic skills, and background knowledge. It is important to collect this type of information so that it can inform and guide your instructional decisions throughout the year.

At the beginning of the year, especially in your first year of teaching, individual assessment can appear to be an overwhelming and impossible task. Finding the time to sit with individual students for a period of time is difficult until classroom routines and procedures are established. Therefore, allow time, say two weeks, to get your classroom running smoothly before you try any individual assessments. This does not mean you won't be noting what your students know through observation or whole-class assessment activities like those in this chapter.

It is also important to note that it usually takes a couple of weeks for K–1 students to feel comfortable in the school environment. Your assessment information will be more accurate when you have allowed this time for adjustment.

It is important to collect different kinds of information on each student throughout the year to help you document growth. The important types of information you collect on each student should include the following:

◆ Samples of student work kept on a regular basis
◆ Anecdotal records of your observations of students' involvement in learning activities
◆ Individual academic pre-assessments of unit objectives as well as summative assessments at the end of each unit

The following are some considerations about assessment:

◆ Attempt to assess only what will be useful to you for planning instruction, reporting to parents, and meeting district requirements.
◆ Expect to assess skills at least once a quarter in addition to the beginning of the year, not all at once.
◆ Be familiar with the report card form, the parent conference form, and so on, to be sure you assess what you are expected to report.
◆ Try to do the assessments yourself. The process a student goes through in answering a question is often more instructive to you than the answer.
◆ In intermediate grades, tell the students what you will be looking for. Eventually, students can participate in the process of establishing assessment criteria.

Getting Started

Have all the assessment materials organized in one spot to take advantage of spare moments. Prepare a box or Ziploc bag with all the materials you will need (e.g., for K–1, pieces of construction paper of all the colors, shapes, counters, alphabet cards, sequence cards, numbers) to test the objectives you are required to report. Include individual student record sheets, all student materials, a pen, and stopwatch for timing fluency in the box or folder.

Anecdotal Records: K–6

Anecdotal records help you focus on individual students on a regular basis. You should plan on spending at least part of each day focusing on five to six children and writing your observations about what they are doing and saying, what they are interested in, and so on. If you observe five or six students a day, you will be observing each child once a week. Even if you observe only two or three students a day, you will build up an impressive record over the year.

Think through your daily schedule to find a few minutes here and there that you could devote to observation. Many times, the task of keeping anecdotal records organized defeats teachers, and they give up on keeping them. Following are several ideas for how to organize the process. Choose one that fits your style.

♦ Make a notebook with dividers for all students. Carry binder paper on your clipboard. Put the child's name and the date at the top of the page and record your observations. File the binder paper in the notebook at the end of the day. Or eliminate filing at the end of the day by carrying the binder with you and writing in it directly.

♦ Make a file box for index cards with a divider for each student. Each day, make a file card for the children you will be observing, including the date. Carry the file cards on a clipboard and make your notes on them. File the cards at the end of the day.

♦ Purchase peel-off address labels and print out a copy of the students' names with the date on the labels, or hand write each name and date. Carry them on a clipboard and record your observation. At the end of the day, peel off the labels and put them in the students' folders. You will know all the students have been assessed once the labels have been used. Just print out new labels and start again.

Making anecdotal records a part of your daily routine will pay off when it comes to parent conference time as well as help you understand the development of each student in your classroom.

Samples of Student Work

K–1. Plan to keep student work on a regular basis—once a week if possible. Be sure to date the work. Types of student work you might want to keep include self-portraits, writing samples, art projects, easel paintings, photocopies of journal entries, photocopies of pages read to you (with errors marked), and reproductions of math work. File the same entry for each student during any given week (e.g., file a self-portrait for everybody during Week 1, a writing sample during Week 2, a painting in Week 3, a math paper in Week 4, then start again with a self-portrait). That way, you will build up a compilation of similar types of samples that you can use to document growth or pinpoint areas of need.

Grades 2–6. Make two folders for every student in your class (or have students make them the first day): a reading–writing folder and a math folder. These folders should be set up in a box file in alphabetical order. You will use these folders to collect student work to use for assessment purposes and to document students' growth throughout the year. They will be useful for parent conferences, referrals, and report cards. Don't attempt to save every piece of student work. Students may decide at the end of the month their best two or three pieces, or you may choose a variety of kinds of work to save.

What goes into the student folders? Assignments you have coded SF (for student folder) in advance, any assessments, student or parent questionnaires, and any significant pieces of student work that demonstrate growth or need.

Making an Assessment Rubric

After giving the students an academic pre-assessment like some of the baseline assessments in this chapter or one before a particular unit of study, you need to know what to do with it. Student samples are filled with information that can help you make sound instructional decisions. You will be dividing the papers into three piles: one for papers that demonstrate emerging qualities, one with skills you have determined as capable, and the last pile is for papers demonstrating advanced skills. Since this is a pre-assessment, it is possible that many of the papers might fall into the emerging pile. That information alone tells you what needs to be taught. If many of the papers fall into the capable and advanced pile, this information may not need to be taught or you might need to determine extension activities. Next, look at the papers in the emerging pile and brainstorm ways you can address those learning needs. What kinds of errors are made? Do you need to re-teach the whole class or a small group? Are the errors misunderstandings that could be cleared up in a mini-lesson or something more fundamental?

Assessment is a critical part of your classroom. Unless you know your students' interests and abilities, you cannot meet their needs with an appropriate curriculum. Spending some time getting to know your students through observation, samples of work, and assessment of skills will give you more confidence in how much your students really do grow and change.

ASSESSMENT FORMS

Checklist for Oral Reading

Assessment of oral reading should be done with students reading individually to you, either during silent reading time or in a private conference. If you do any writing as a student reads, it should be as unobtrusive as possible, and you should assure the student you have confidence in him or her and that you are just making notes to help you remember how well he or she reads. Information may be checked off on this form or listed later in an anecdotal record.

Reading material_____   Date_____

Reading Fluency

[ ] Very slowly, sounding out each word
[ ] Word by word
[ ] Quickly in phrases

Decoding Strategies for Unknown Words

[ ] Looks for biggest known chunks (morphemes)
[ ] Sounds out syllable by syllable
[ ] Sounds out letter by letter

Note particular decoding errors, group errors.

Punctuation

[ ] Ignores punctuation
[ ] Stops for periods but shows no expression
[ ] Expression appropriate to punctuation

General

[ ] Reading material held too close or too far away (eye problem?)
[ ] Uncomfortable, didn't like reading
[ ] Doesn't respond appropriately to comprehension checks

How Challenging Is This Book for the Student?

[ ] Very easy
[ ] Enjoyable
[ ] Challenging
[ ] Frustrating

Oral Reading and Comprehension Assessment

Find three different consecutive levels of text. Copy a selection from each, or use those provided by your district. Have students read a single copy of each passage; have multiple copies for yourself to use for recording. Have the text header show the student's name and date, and allow space for tracking individual errors and scoring.

Oral Reading Miscue Code

Student	Teacher Response	Record (Example)
Reads correctly	Listen, follow along	Nothing
Misreads a word	Write the error above the word on copy	Sleep Slept
Omits a word	Cross out the word	~~As~~
Adds a word	Insert the word with a caret	ever When^ she arrives
Doesn't know a word, looks to you for assistance	Tell the student the word (no prompting), write "T" above	T Apartment
Self-corrects an error	Write "SC" above the word	SC Tight
Repeats or rereads a word, phrase, or sentence	Write "R" above the word or, for a phrase or sentence, indicate where she or he began rereading	R Repairman _____ R A jukebox repairman
Uses phonics to sound out words	Write "PH" above the word	PH Trade

First, allow time for student to read the passage silently. When he or she reads the passage aloud, note errors using the Oral Reading Miscue Code. Ask the series of reading comprehension questions. When completed, thank the student, score his or her performance according to the comprehension rubric, and call on the next student. Information gleaned from these assessments will help you determine the instruction needed for both individuals and groups of students. It will also help determine each student's appropriate literature level. This method, when used regularly, ensures that students are guided by accurate information about their developmental needs.

Reading Comprehension Questions

Student: _____   Date: _____

Book Title: _____   Book Level: _____

Ask the student to read and answer the following questions. Let the student know he or she may refer back to the text, if necessary.

◆ What was this story about? _____

_____

_____

_____

◆ Describe a character in the story. How did that person look and act? How did other characters react to him or her? How do you know?

_____

_____

_____

_____

◆ What would be a good title for the story, and why? _____

_____

_____

_____

◆ If the story were continued, what might happen next? _____

_____

_____

◆ What was the most important event in the story? Why? _____

_____

_____

_____

Reading Comprehension Rubric

Student: _____   Date: _____

Book Title: _____   Book Level: _____

	1	2	3
A	Retold story out of sequence, with some incorrect information about events and when they occurred	Retold major events of story in correct sequence, with few details	Retold story, in sequence, clearly identifying and describing the beginning, middle and end of story—may have identified a problem and solution
B	Described a character with few details, omitted evidence to support opinions	Described some aspects of the character, omitted evidence to support opinions	Described a character in detail and supported opinions with evidence from the text
C	No ideas for a new title, or title does not fit story	Appropriate title	Creative title with justification
D	No prediction, or the prediction is not a logical extension of story	Reasonable prediction	Reasonable, descriptive prediction that clearly defines in detail what might happen next
E	Identifies an event that may not be a key event, does not support opinion with evidence	Identifies a key event and gives a plausible reason for the selection based on facts in the story	Identifies a key event and clearly describes why it is a key event, connecting literal and inferential information found in text

Other Quick Reading-Writing Assessments

Five-Finger Test

This is a student self-assessment of independent reading level. Teach your students this quick method of determining their independent reading level early in the year:

1. Choose a book.

2. Choose a page and read silently to yourself.

3. Place a finger on each unknown word on one page.

4. When five fingers have been placed on a single page, you may decide that the book is too difficult for you to read alone.

5. Choose another book and begin again.

6. List in your reading record the book you decide to read.

Quick Sorts

Quick sorts are short, quick tests, usually for decoding or sight word reading ability. They are useful for a quick snapshot of where individual students are in these areas and will help you in grouping students to work on decoding and sight word skills. They should not be used to determine a child's reading placement for the rest of the year. Some examples of quick sorts are, for English reading, the San Diego Quick Assessment and the Slosson; for Spanish reading, the Santillana Quick Placement.

Assessing Student Writing

During the first month of school you will want to collect samples of several types of writing from students. These might include creative stories (from the Wiggly Line worksheet), letters (their letters to you), factual writing ("Who Lives at My House"), reflective writing (journals), and creating questions (various interview activities). Saving samples of each of these over time will allow you to see whether growth is taking place in both content and form. You won't have the time to record a detailed analysis of all the information that each piece can reveal, so you will need to scan for particular aspects that will inform your immediate instruction and help students focus on goals for themselves.

A simple way to do this is to sort the writing samples into three stacks: (a) those papers that show developing or emergent qualities; (b) those papers that show capable writing techniques; and (c) those papers that show strong qualities. See the *Writing Rubric and Checklist for Writing Assessment* for samples of check sheets that you could use to determine general writing deficiencies within the class so as to instruct your lessons. It can also be used for individual written work to give the students feedback.

Monthly Writing Sample

On the first day of every month, have students write one page of their best writing. You can either have students save these pages in their writing folders or keep the pages posted on a bulletin board, with the current month's work stapled on top.

Checklist for Writing Assessment

This is a checklist for you to use in looking at student work and for notation on the anecdotal record form, not for red-penciling student work. Use this list also to create student proofreading self-assessments. Do not look at every paper for every aspect of writing. Use the information you gather to plan what lessons you will teach. Is it something the whole class will need or just a small group?

Content of Writing, Narrative (any fictional story)

[ ] Is there a sequence—beginning, middle, and end?
[ ] Does a plot develop—problem, response, action, outcome? Is it believable, logical, exciting?
[ ] Are there interesting characters? (Good description?)
[ ] Does the setting add to the story? (Good description?)

Content of Writing, Expository (any nonfiction explanatory writing)

[ ] Was an organizational structure used in prewriting? (Matrix, hierarchy, web, outline, list?)
[ ] Are there supporting facts?
[ ] Are there smooth transitions between statements, paragraphs?

Mechanics of Writing

[ ] Was appropriate form used? (Paragraphs, letter format, title?)
[ ] Are there trends in the kinds of grammar errors made?
[ ] Was correct punctuation or capitalization used consistently?
[ ] Is the sentence structure correct? Is there space between words?

Spelling

[ ] Are there phonetic problems, families of words?
[ ] Are high-frequency words spelled correctly?
[ ] Are misspellings due to oral or aural language problems?
[ ] Is your spelling program covering the errors?

(Spelling programs are a question you'll need to address at your school site. If you don't feel the current program is meeting your students' needs, you will need to be able to articulate an alternative to parents and administration clearly before changing your approach.)

Penmanship

[ ] Are there problems with basic letter formation?
[ ] Is motor coordination a problem?
[ ] Is neatness a problem? Is there a difference between a draft and a published copy?
[ ] What could the student do to improve his or her penmanship?

Self-Editing Checklist

_____ I have read my work to myself both silently and aloud.

_____ I have read my work to _____ (classmate/s)

_____ Capitalization: I have checked that every sentence and name starts with a capital letter.

_____ Punctuation: I put periods (.), question marks (?), or exclamation points (!) at the end of each sentence.

_____ Spelling: I underlined words I think are misspelled.

[ ] I tried different ways to spell them.

[ ] I used a dictionary.

[ ] I asked a classmate.

_____ My story has a beginning, a middle, and an end.

Lista de control para la auto-corrección

_____ Leí mi trabajo a mi mismo en voz alta y en silencio.

_____ Le leí mi trabajo a _____ (compañero/a de clase).

_____ Mayúsculas: Comprobé que cada frase y nombre empieza con mayúscula.

_____ Marcas de puntuación: Puse puntos (.), signos de interrogación (?), o signos de admiración (!) al final de cada frase.

_____ Ortografía: Subrayé las palabras que creo que están mal escritas.

[ ] Probé otras maneras de escribirlas.

[ ] Usé un diccionario.

[ ] Pregunté a un compañero de clase.

_____ Mi cuento tiene comienzo, parte media, y final.

Writer's Workshop Observation Guide

When students are working on writing, you will find your class in various stages of the writing process. You will want a simple, efficient way to keep track of what students are working on and where their strengths and needs are. This checklist is designed for assessment of each of the stages of the writing process. As students work, walk around with the Writer's Workshop Class Profile form (or something similar) and make notes on their progress in the particular stages they are working on in the writing process. If you have 30 students, you will need to comment on only six each day to cover the entire class by the end of a week. This will leave you plenty of time for individual conferences and other supportive work.

In all stages of the process, it may be useful to note whether students are on task, who they are working with, and what their attitudes seem to be about what they are doing, as well as any areas that you work on with a student. Here are some suggestions to think about at each stage:

Prewriting: Does the student demonstrate organizational skills, brainstorming, mind mapping, outlining, note taking? Does the student have difficulty in this phase? What might the obstacles be?

Drafting: Does the student write fluently? (Note the number of words or lines written.) Does spelling get in the way? Is the student comfortable inventing spelling? (Note topics the student writes on.)

Revision: See the content sections of the Checklist for Writing Assessment for possible areas of revision. What motivates the student to revise? Does the student find his or her own areas of weakness? Whose feedback does the student value?

Editing: See the mechanics section of the Checklist for Writing Assessment. Does the student become overwhelmed by mechanical problems?

Publishing: What form does the student choose for publishing? (Note how long this process takes and the student's attitude toward publishing the work.)

Remember, the point is not to write copious notes on students but simply to jot down quick observations that will indicate to you where students are and what they were doing on the day that you checked in with them. The Writers Workshop Class Profile is an example of an observation form.

Writer's Workshop Class Profile

Codes for stages: PW = Prewriting, D = Drafting, R = Revising, E = Editing,
P = Publishing

Week of _____

Names of Students	Topic or Story	Comments (Stage Appropriate)

Student Self-Assessment

Materials: Enough teacher-made worksheets for all students, pencils
Grouping: Whole class
Approximate Time: 20–30 minutes

Directions:

1. Make your own worksheet or use one of the following examples of a self-assessment.

2. Look over the assessment, go over it with the class. Brainstorm ideas for responses.

3. Pass out the worksheets and explain this activity to the students. For example, you might say something such as:

   The more we know about ourselves, the better choices we can make. This activity will help you reflect on how you learn and the kind of activities you like to do. I will collect and read these worksheets, but the information will remain private. The more thought you put into your answers, the more helpful this activity will be. You will have approximately fifteen minutes to complete the worksheet. I will collect the papers when everyone is finished. If you finish early, you may silently read a book.

4. Give the signal to begin, and then circulate around the room, keeping the students on task. You may want to fill out one of the worksheets yourself.

5. When everyone has finished, give the zero-noise signal and collect the papers.

Closure: Ask such questions as, "Did anyone find a question difficult to answer? Which one? Why do you think it was difficult?" (Be prepared to volunteer your own responses. You are modeling for the students that the classroom is a safe place to share ideas and feelings.) Also, be sure to say, "Thank you for your honest responses. They will help me know you better."

Read the worksheets carefully. The responses will give you insight into your students' behavior and how they learn. Some students will be able to analyze their feelings better than others. Keep the worksheets in individual student folders. Do this activity periodically throughout the school year or just once more at the end of the year, and let the students compare their responses.

Student Interest Survey

Name _____

Answer each statement as best as you can.

1. I like school. _____

_____

2. I have many friends. _____

_____

3. I have a close friend. _____

_____

4. I'm good at art. _____

_____

5. I like science. _____

_____

6. I'm good at sports. _____

_____

7. My favorite subject is _____

_____

8. My least favorite subject is _____

_____

9. I'm good at _____

_____

10. I could improve in _____

_____

Evaluación Personal del Estudiante

Nombre _____

Escriba un oración por cada uno de los siguientes.

1. A mí me gusta la escuela. _____

_____

2. Tengo muchos amigos. _____

_____

3. Tengo un amigo favorito. _____

_____

4. A mí me gusta el arte. _____

_____

5. A mí me gustan las ciencias. _____

_____

6. Soy un buen deportista. _____

_____

7. La materia que más me gusta es _____

_____

8. La materia que menos me gusta es _____

_____

9. Soy bueno en cuanto a _____

_____

10. Yo podría mejorar en _____

_____

Learning Preferences and Study Skills

Name _____

	YES	NO
1. I am a responsible person.		
2. I am dependable.		
3. I am cooperative.		
4. I turn my work in on time.		
5. I listen and follow directions.		
6. I am a fair person.		
7. I use my time wisely.		
8. I like to work alone.		
9. I like to work with a friend.		
10. I need to work in a quiet room.		
11. Noise doesn't bother me when I work.		
12. I like to get my work done quickly.		
13. I wait to the last minute to turn in my work.		
14. I like to build and make things.		
15. I like to hear stories read aloud.		
16. I understand things better if there are pictures.		
17. I can hear a tune and remember it.		
18. I like to spend time outside in nature.		
19. I am good with numbers.		

Preferencias de Aprendizaje y Capacidades de Estudiar

Nombre _____

	SI	NO
1. Soy una persona responsable.		
2. Soy digno de confianza.		
3. Soy cooperativo.		
4. Entrego la tarea a tiempo.		
5. Escucho y sigo las direcciones.		
6. Soy una persona justa.		
7. Uso el tiempo sabiamente.		
8. Me gusta trabajar solo.		
9. Me gusta trabajar con un amigo.		
10. Necesito que un cuarto sea silencioso para concentrarme.		
11. Me gusta un poco de ruido cuando estoy trabajando.		
12. Me gusta completar mi trabajo rápidamente.		
13. Espero hasta el ultimo minuto para entregar mi trabajo.		
14. Me gusta construir o hacer cosas.		
15. Me gusta que me lean cuentos en voz alta.		
16. Entiendo las cosas mejor si hay dibujos.		
17. Puedo oír una melodía y recordarla.		
18. Me gusta pasar tiempo afuera en la naturaleza.		
19. Tengo facilidad con los números.		

What I Think About Reading

Name _____ Date _____

1. How do I feel about reading?

2. How much time do I read and when do I do it?

3. When I can read anything I choose, I read

4. I like to read books and stories about

5. The best books or stories I have ever read were

6. The things I don't like about reading are

7. What I would like to do in reading this year is

8. This is how I can become a better reader

Lo Que Yo Opino de la Lectura

Nombre _____ Fecha _____

1. ¿Cómo me siento acerca de la lectura?

2. ¿Cuánto tiempo paso leyendo? ¿Cuándo leo?

3. Cuando puedo leer cualquier cosa, yo escojo

4. Me gusta leer los libros y cuentos acerca de

5. Los mejores libros o cuentos que yo he leído son

6. Lo que no me gusta acerca de la lectura es

7. Lo que yo quisiera hacer este año en la clase de lectura es

8. Voy a ser mejorar mi capacidad en lectura en la siguiente manera

What I Think About Writing

Name _____ Date _____

1. How do I feel about writing?

2. The kinds of writing I enjoy most are

3. The hardest thing about writing is

4. The best things I've ever written were

5. Some of the things I would like to do better in my writing are

6. Some of the things I do well in my stories are

Lo Que Pienso Acerca de la Escritura

Nombre _____ Fecha _____

1. ¿Cómo me siento acerca de la escritura?

2. De la siguiente lista, el tema sobre el que más me gustaría escribir es

3. Lo que más me cuesta a la hora de escribir es

4. Las mejores cosas que he escrito son

5. Algunas de las cosas que quisiera mejorar cuando escribo son

6. Algunas de las cosas que hago bien en mis cuentos son

What I Think About Math

Name _____ Date _____

1. After a math assessment, I feel

    _____ nervous about how I did.

    _____ confident and proud about how much I knew.

    _____ just okay.

2. When new math ideas are introduced, I usually

    _____ pick them up right away.

    _____ need some extra help.

    _____ feel lost.

3. My parents (or caregivers)

    _____ are good at math and like it.

    _____ tell me they never were good at math.

    _____ I don't know whether they like math or not.

4. My favorite kind of math is

    _____ computation.

    _____ problem solving.

    _____ neither of these. I really don't like math.

5. I think

    _____ boys perform better than girls in math.

    _____ girls perform better than boys in math.

    _____ there's no difference between boys and girls in math.

6. When I think about my future career, I might

    _____ need to use a lot of math.

    _____ choose a career that doesn't use math at all.

    _____ figure I can learn whatever math I'll need to use.

7. Something that helps me learn math

8. My favorite type of math is

Lo Que Yo Pienso De Las Matemáticas

Nombre _____ Fecha _____

1. Después de un examin de matemática siento

    _____ anciosa de los resultos.

    _____ con confianza y orgullosa de lo que sabia.

    _____ así, así.

2. Quando se introducen nuevos ideas de matemática

    _____ yo los pego imediatamente.

    _____ necesito mas ayuda.

    _____ siento perdido.

3. Mis padres/o familia

    _____ tienen capacidades y les gustan matemáticas.

    _____ me dicen que no son buenos en hacer matemática.

    _____ no sé se les gustan o no.

4. El tipo de matemática que me gusta mas es

    _____ calculación.

    _____ resolviendo problemas.

    _____ ni uno ni otro. No me gusta.

5. Yo pienso que

    _____ muchachos tienen mas capaz en matemática que las muchachas.

    _____ muchachas tienen mas capaz en matemática que muchachos.

    _____ no hay una diferencia entre muchachas y muchachos en su capaz de hacer matemática.

6. Cuando pienso en mi carrera de futuro. Tal vez

    _____ necesito usar mucho matemática.

    _____ escojerá una carrera que no se usa matemática.

    _____ pienso que podria aprender qualquier.

7. Algo que me ayuda aprender matemática

8. Mi predilecto tipo de matemática es

Who Am I?

Materials: Prompts
Grouping: Whole class, lined up horizontally
Approximate Time: 20 minutes

Introduction: Ask students to silently stand in a horizontal line (on a piece of tape). Tell students they will be moving after each statement, depending on how they feel they agree or disagree with the statement. The *far-left* side of the line will be for those who disagree with the statement; the *far-right* side is for those who agree. Ask what students will need to keep in mind when moving from place to place.

Posing the following statements, have students move as appropriate for *agreement* and *disagreement*:

- At home, I read a lot.
- Math is one of my favorite subjects.
- If I could, I'd practice art all day.
- I really look forward to PE.
- I consider myself a writer-author.
- I am very comfortable using the computer.
- I love to talk.
- I like to build and fix things.
- I like to sing.
- This year, I would love to be in a play.

Have students take their seats, several at a time by calling those born in January and December; progress through the year.

When all the students are seated, put the statements on an overhead projector and ask students to write descriptions of themselves in relation to the statements. Ask them to add other details about their feelings toward school or academic tasks.

3

Routines and Procedures

Consistent daily routines will help students feel comfortable and know what to expect. Clear procedures will help students know exactly what behavior is expected in the various learning situations you create.

This chapter provides you with sage advice on classroom management's cardinal rules and key strategies to gain student attention with a "Freeze and Listen" code, as well as advice on how to set procedures for clean up, various lesson formats, and class meetings. This chapter also will provide you with strategies regarding behavior for both promoting good behavior and correcting misbehavior, as well as some suggestions for rewards systems. It also provides daily routines for silent reading, read alouds, journals, literature logs, and calendars, as well as some specific suggestions to include English learners in your activities and provide them access to the content in your classroom.

CARDINAL RULES OF CLASSROOM MANAGEMENT

Remember the cardinal rules of classroom management: *Model, practice, focus on the positive, and be consistent.*

The following sections outline procedures for various classroom management areas that must be in place for you to be successful. These are the "hidden systems" you may not have been aware of in your observations of classrooms or in your student teaching. We urge you to read them carefully, implement them as outlined, and keep at them until your students have learned them.

Creating procedures helps you think through your behavioral expectations for any given activity. That way, you are able to communicate those expectations clearly to the students and thus prevent disruptions. You can either tell the students your expectations for a specific procedure or have the class develop them under your guidance.

FREEZE AND LISTEN

This is a must. You need to decide what signal you will use to notify your students that they must stop, look, and listen to an adult. This could be a bell, a chord on the piano, a note sounded on a xylophone, a hand signal—whatever you choose. In kindergarten and first grade, it is useful to have the students do an accompanying body motion when they hear the signal (e.g., hands in the air, hands on head).

Starting from the first day, at the first transition, you must model, role-play, and practice this procedure over and over. It is critical that all the adults in the room model the desired behavior along with the students. At the first class meeting, explain the procedure—a visual is helpful (e.g., a picture of a bell, above a stop sign, above big eyes, above big ears) to use as you explain (see Figure 3.1). At the first whole-group meeting, you might do the following to model the procedure (note that the language in this example is designed for a K–2 class; you will need to adapt it for grades 3–6).

Figure 3.1   Sample Freeze-and-Listen

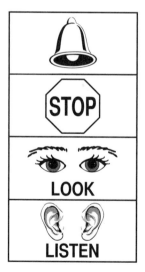

Say, "Today, we're going to practice what we do when we hear this sound. First, Alicia [the teacher's aide] and I will show you what to do." You then choose a child to be the "teacher" and whisper in his or her ear what he or she is to do—for example, let you talk and color for a few moments, and then ring a bell. You pretend to be coloring and talking with Alicia until your "teacher" rings the bell or gives whatever freeze-and-listen signal you have chosen. At that point, you must model exactly what you want the kids to do: *Freeze and look at the "teacher."*

Next, call up a small group of students to role-play what you and your aide just did. Your aide can take the role-play group away to review what they are going to do while you give the others the task of being the observers and watching for the proper behavior. Have the role-players pretend to be busy. Make your freeze-and-listen signal, and praise, praise, praise when they comply. Encourage the audience to praise also.

Now, you're ready to have the whole class role-play. Have them stay in the circle and pretend to be busy coloring, talking quietly to their neighbors. Make your freeze-and-listen signal. If you have classroom assistance, instruct them to go to noncompliers and quietly remind them of the procedure. You should focus on giving positive praise to those who are complying and to the whole class when all comply.

Review the procedure with the students using the visual. This activity should take ten to fifteen minutes and should be followed by something active.

This procedure will have to be practiced often—at every transition for the first week or so. That means you should continue to have your aide or family volunteer involved, continue to praise, and continue to redirect those students having a hard time learning the procedure. Spending time and energy putting this procedure firmly in place will pay huge dividends later.

CLEANUP

In an active, interactive classroom, your students must be responsible for the maintenance of the environment. Several different types of cleanup need to be considered.

Individual Responsibilities

The rule is to clean up after yourself. During the first few days of school, include this in any modeling you do. For example, if you are doing a cut-and-paste art project and are explaining the how to, be sure to include the how to of cleanup in your explanation—where to put your scissors when you've finished, where scraps go, and so on. As you review the project after completion, make a special note to compliment the students' efforts at cleanup. In kindergarten and first grade, it is effective to start a chant or song to accompany cleanup. For example, to the tune of "The Farmer in the Dell," you can sing, "It's time to clean up now, it's time to clean up now. Heigh ho the derry-o, it's time to clean up now. *Es hora de limpiar, es hora de limpiar. Que viva la escuela, es hora de limpiar."*

The success of cleanup will depend on your having clearly marked areas for supplies that are easily accessible to the students. Remember the decisions you made about materials. Make sure the students know their responsibilities. Students must know what to do after they have cleaned up their own work spaces (e.g., sit at the whole-group area and wait quietly or go to their seat and look at a book).

Classroom Responsibilities

These cleanup duties involve such tasks as keeping the book corner neat, washing the tables, and taking the roll to the office. It is helpful to have a "jobs chart" that lists the tasks that need to be done on a daily basis but in which not everyone needs to participate. Such a chart could take many different forms (a sample format is shown in Figure 3.2); however, the most important aspects are that students are trained in what the jobs entail, that jobs are rotated in a fair manner, and that you are consistent in making students accountable for completing their jobs. Some possible classroom jobs for students are library monitor, light monitor, office monitor, leader of cleanup, leader of games, leader for the flag salute, pencils monitor, and line leader.

Figure 3.2 Jobs Chart

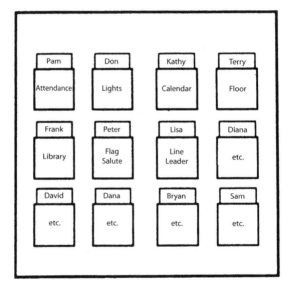

The students can participate in the development of the jobs chart by brainstorming what jobs need to be done. Don't do this the first day of school but shortly thereafter. Again, role-play, model, and reinforce what is expected for each job. This could be done as an inclusion activity in which you divide the class into groups and have each group learn one job and teach it to a partner.

Special Project Cleanup Responsibilities

When you plan a messy activity, consider how you can involve the students in cleanup. Often, the cleanup of these projects can fall to you or your aide.

Include cleanup procedures in the explanation of the project and review them with students before beginning to work on the project.

PROCEDURES FOR LESSONS, GROUPS, AND ROTATIONS

Teacher-Directed Whole-Class Lesson

Procedures for a teacher-directed lesson with the whole class may vary depending on the kind of lesson involved. You may want to require that desks are cleared off or that certain materials are out on the desks. Use your freeze-and-listen signal to get attention.

You want to have clear procedures for the kind of attention you expect (chairs turned to face you, eyes looking at you, students may be drawing while you are talking). Think them through, and make them clear and reasonable (for example, consider what to tell students to do if they cannot see or hear you or if they need to sharpen a pencil). Spell the procedures out clearly.

Use positive language when writing your procedures. Say what you *want* the students to do, not what they should not do ("Listen quietly" instead of "Don't talk"). Make the procedures short (use as few words as needed to get the information across), and make them few in number. Write them on a chart, and keep them on hand to refer to. Now you are ready to teach the procedures to the class. Discuss each one, model what it looks like, and show what it doesn't look like. Reinforce the procedures using positive praise. The use of thoughtfully worded and clearly taught procedures is the foundation to your classroom management.

Rules and *procedures* are not the same things. Rules apply to all students all of the time. "Be respectful," "Use your words, not your fists," and "No toys or candy at school," are all examples of rules. Whether it is during reading centers or a math lesson, the rules do not change. Procedures, on the other hand, vary according to the lesson or activity. "Raise your hand and wait to be called on," is a good procedure for a teacher-led lesson but not for paired interviews.

Sample Procedure Chart for a Teacher-Directed Whole-Class Lesson

1. Clear your desk and stay in your seat.
2. One person talks at a time.
3. Raise your hand to speak.
4. Focus on (look at!) the speaker.
5. Follow teacher directions.

1. Quita todo de encima del escritorio y quédate en tu asiento.
2. Que hable una sola persona a la vez.
3. Levanta la mano para hablar.
4. Fíjate en el orador. (Mírale al orador.)
5. Sigue las instrucciones de la maestra.

Teacher-Directed Whole Group on the Floor or Rug

In kindergarten, most whole-group instruction is done with the students sitting on the floor. In first and second grade, this is still true, but some instruction is done with students sitting at their seats. For this type of instruction, see the procedures outlined earlier.

For whole-group floor procedures, the following should be practiced from the first day of school:

- Students should know where and how to sit. Some teachers prefer a circle arrangement. If you choose this arrangement, mark the circle on the floor with tape to delineate its size and where students should sit.

- Some teachers prefer a group with an undefined shape or rows. If you use rows, again, mark the rug or floor with tape. For an undefined arrangement, you need to delineate the boundaries of the group space in some way—often, furniture will do this, but you must make it clear to your students what is out of bounds (e.g., being under a piece of furniture or behind a chair).

- It is important to practice the "how to" of sitting on the floor. Don't use the term *Indian style*—avoid stereotyping. Instead, show the students the cross-legged position expected at floor time. Use a chant such as "I sit on the floor by myself, crisscross," to remind them of the expectation instead of singling out individuals. Again, use your aide to individually help those having a hard time.

- Decide and tell your students how you expect them to respond to questions or to join in discussions—raise hands, shout out, wait until someone has finished speaking, etc. This may vary from activity to activity but should be made clear at the beginning of each activity.

Small-Group Teacher-Directed Lesson

In this format, the teacher will be working with a small group while the rest of the class is working either independently or cooperatively in other small groups with learning assistants (adults or cross-age helpers). Before working with a small group, set the rules for the other groups in the class—what if they need to use the bathroom, don't have a pencil, or have a question? All problems should have procedures so that, short of a minor disaster, you are free to work with your small group.

In your small group, set procedures for how students are to come to the work area, what they should bring, what transition activity they are to do while waiting for the directed group to start, how they are to respond in a discussion (informally, raising hands, and so on), and if supplies are at the workstation, who distributes them, who collects them, and what procedures are to be followed in leaving the workstation.

Sample Procedure Chart for a Small-Group Teacher-Directed Lesson

1. Come quietly to the group with materials.
2. Follow directions on the board for transition activity.
3. Give attention to the speaker in the group.
4. Raise your hand to speak unless it is open discussion.
5. Clean up before leaving.
6. Return quietly to your own seat and begin work.
1. Ven calladito a tu grupo con tus materiales.
2. Sigue las instrucciones en el pizarrón para la actividad transitoria.
3. Fija tu atención en el orador del grupo.
4. Levanta la mano para hablar, a menos que sea una discusión abierta.
5. Limpia la estación antes de partir.
6. Regresa calladito a tu propio escritorio y comienza a trabajar.

Small-Group Rotations

Usually, a teacher sets up some kind of rotation system to ensure that he or she sees each student on a regular basis and has the opportunity to provide direct instruction to small groups. It is critical to train your students in the rotation system you choose before doing any in-depth content.

You need to think through the organization of any rotation times you will schedule. For example, during an hour-long language arts period, you might want to see two groups for a half hour each. That would mean that in a class with four groups, you would see each student every other day. Or, you may wish to see each group every day. Therefore, you would need a two-hour block for language arts or you would see each group for only fifteen minutes. Once you have decided for how long you will see each group, you have other decisions to make:

- ♦ What kind of adult help do you have? What will their responsibilities be? What kind of system will you use to tell them what to do?
- ♦ How will the students be grouped: by language, by ability, heterogeneously by language?
- ♦ What will the non-teacher-directed activities be: journals, spelling, workbooks, handwriting, listening center, oral reading?
- ♦ Will you use cross-age tutors? What activities are appropriate for them to work with?
- ♦ Will students always rotate with the same groups, or will they be divided differently for independent workstations?
- ♦ Where will you meet with students? Where will the aides, tutors, and family volunteers meet with students?

Once you have made these decisions, you can begin to formulate a plan. Sit down with a piece of paper, a class list, and your assessment information, if you wish. On a blank piece of paper, make a grid with the number of rotations you will have down one side and the activities you have across the top.

For example:

Table 3.1 Rotation Grid

	Teacher's Aide-Directed Lesson	**Independent Cut-and-Paste Game**	**Listening Book and Tape**
8:30–9:00			
9:00–9:30			
9:30–10:00			
10:00–10:30			

This would be a four-group rotation, with the teacher seeing each student every day. Once you have your time schedule and activities down, you can begin to group your students. We recommend heterogeneous grouping as opposed to skill-level grouping.

In a bilingual situation, the only limitation during a language arts time will be language of instruction. You will need to have your students in groups based on whether they are learning literacy concepts in English or Spanish. In math, social studies, and other subjects, however, languages may be mixed.

Divide your class as nearly as you can into four equally numbered groups. Name each group (number, color, animal; see Table 3.1). This is just for the purposes of figuring out the rotation. Once groups have been established, a good team-building activity is for them to name themselves. You can then begin to fill in the rotation scheme.

What colors would go in the listening column in Table 3.1? If you thought Green, Blue, Red, and then Yellow, you're on your way to developing systems. This is the simplest system; students stay with the same group throughout the rotation schedule. This is a good place to start.

Now that you know what will happen, you need to teach the rotation and what is expected at each "station." Plan on spending at least two weeks being the facilitator in this learning by easing into a full rotation system. In other words, don't plan to spend time with your small group—you will be roaming, praising, answering questions, keeping students on task, and so on. You will only be frustrated if you try to do a lesson as well. Have independent work for your group to do. The following procedure outlines a sample strategy for introducing rotation centers:

Table 3.2 Sample Rotation Grid

	Teacher	**Aide**	**Independent**	**Listening**
8:30-9:00	Blue	Red	Yellow	?
9:00-9:30	Red	Yellow	Green	?
9:30-10:00	Yellow	Green	Blue	?
10:00-10:30	Green	Blue	Red	?

♦ Prepare a chart with the students' names listed under the colors of their groups or written on construction paper of the colors of their groups. Post the chart near your whole-group meeting area. (For kindergartners, you could also add a photocopied picture of each child next to his or her name.)

♦ Show the chart to the students at whole-group time. Explain to them how to find which group they belong to. Have several students come up and point to their names. Have the whole group shout out these students' group colors.

♦ Say, "All students in the Blue Group stand up quietly." Read off the names from your chart and have the students sit down as you call their names. Continue for each group. (In kindergarten, hand out colored-yarn necklaces for the students to wear as they determine their group colors. You can use these for a few days to help you and the students learn the groups.)

Now, hopefully, everyone knows his or her group. The next step is to work on the rotation scheme. Shorten the time allotted at each station during the first two weeks of practice. A sample strategy follows:

♦ On the first day of practice, have all your students learn what happens at the teacher center. Say, "When it's your turn to work with me, you will come to the horseshoe table in the back of the classroom. While you wait for me to get everyone settled, you will look at one of the books in the blue box." Have one group role-play this for the whole class.

♦ Next, move everyone to the next station. Say, "This is where you will work with Alicia [aide]." Explain all items the students should bring with them when coming to this work area, if any. Move through all the stations in this manner. Do it quickly—only an overview at this time.

Figure 3.3   Rotation Chart

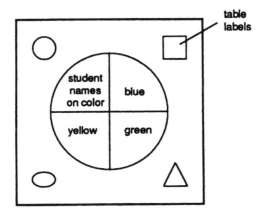

♦ Now, introduce a rotation chart, such as the one shown in Figure 3.3, or an individual "map" to be pasted in each student's work folder, such as those shown in Figure 3.4. In whole group, have the students determine where they go for Rotation 1. At your signal, the Blue Group will go to its assigned area, followed by the Red, Green, and Yellow groups, one at a time. When all groups are at their assigned first rotations, make your freeze-and-listen signal. Wait for complete attention, and then have students determine where they go for the second rotation. Model how to rotate: Walk quietly and quickly to where you go. Do this all together by saying, "Everyone stand up. Point to where you go. Now, walk quietly to Rotation 2." Repeat for Rotations 3 and 4. Give plenty of praise and encouragement.

◆ Now that students are at Rotation 4, have them go back to Rotation 1, and have an activity planned for them to do.

◆ The next day, review the rotation scheme in whole group. Use four students from each of the four groups to model. Start with Rotation 1. Have the four role-play students go to their assigned tables, and have the other students help you review the signal that will tell them to move. Make the signal and say, "Rotation 2." The role-play students should move accordingly. Other students can applaud. Continue role-playing with Rotations 3 and 4.

◆ Now, you're ready to do a full-scale run. Have group activities prepared and at the centers. Activities should be simple. Remember that your small-group activity should be independent. The more responsibility you can give to your students for figuring out what to do, the better. For example, a directions poster for each center will give them visual clues as to what to do. Directions should rely on pictures and words to get the message across.

◆ Encourage your students to ask each other for help. *Do not allow yourself to become the sole keeper of knowledge. Be consistent in not answering the questions that students can ask each other.* Explain to your students that when they have questions, they should first ask themselves, then a friend, before they raise their hands to let you know they have questions. Stress the importance of not interrupting the teacher when he or she is teaching. This is part of developing a love for learning—the most important element in the classroom is having respect for that process.

◆ Dismiss each group in turn to go to Rotation 1. You should roam and give specific praise, help any students who are having a hard time getting started, reinforce work behavior, and so on.

◆ When it is time to move to Rotation 2, make your freeze-and-listen signal. Review cleanup, where they will move, and so on. Say, "You have two minutes to clean up and be ready to move. I will know you are ready to move when I see your whole group sitting quietly with folders in front of you and your eyes on me." Wait until you see that. Then, have everyone get up and move to the next station.

◆ Repeat for Rotations 3 and 4. You will probably need to do this for the entire first week. The goal is to establish this routine clearly so you do not need to be involved and can devote your attention to your small group without interruption. You can expect to be able to do this only if you practice, practice, practice the first few weeks of school.

◆ In kindergarten and first grade, putting soothing music on facilitates calm when returning to whole-group work.

Figure 3.4 Individual Student Rotation "Maps"

John (Blue group)

Rotation	Where	
1	Teacher	□
2	Independent	△
3	Aide	○
4	Listening	⬯

María (Red group)

Rotation	Where	
1	Independent	□
2	Aide	△
3	Listening	○
4	Teacher	⬯

Independent Workers

Spend several weeks training students on independent work. Think through exactly what behaviors will be acceptable during independent work time, and write up a chart explaining these. For instance, will you allow students to talk, to get out of their seats, to ask others for help? What if they need help to sharpen a pencil, get a drink of water, or go to the bathroom? What do they do when they finish their work? Set the procedures, and leave yourself free to monitor behavior. This means that if you're practicing independent time and they need help, you do not help them; instead, you have them follow the procedures that are set up. The following chart has examples of procedures.

Sample Procedure Chart for Independent Workers

1. Work by yourself or with a partner.
2. Focus on the assigned work.
3. Whisper if you need to ask a question.
4. Follow cooperative group procedures if you have a question: (a) Ask yourself, (b) ask a neighbor, (c) ask someone at another table.
5. Do not interrupt the teacher.

1. Trabaja sólo o con un(a) compañero/a.
2. Fíjate en el trabajo asignado.
3. Usa voz baja si tienes que hacer una pregunta.
4. Sigue el proceso de grupos cooperativos si tienes alguna pregunta: (a) Pregúntate, (b) pregúntale a un vecino, (c) pregúntale a alguien en otra mesa.
5. No le interrumpas a la maestra.

Cooperative Learning Groups

Teach a *zero-noise hand signal* before beginning any cooperative groups. When you raise your hand, students are to (a) raise their hands, (b) get quiet, and (c) tap the shoulders of others around them to get quiet. Practice this many times throughout the day over several days before beginning cooperative learning groups.

Positive Praise

Teach words for use in praising one another. Brainstorm words on the board so that students have words of their own to use. Add to the list throughout the year. Keep the list handy for students to refer to. Role-play, practice, and reward usage of praise words.

Individual and Group Rewards

Students will continue to need to be rewarded for individual efforts as well as for group efforts. They should receive rewards for processes, procedures, and activities, as well as for products. Rewards can be anything from verbal praise, smiles, and pats on the back to points, raffles, and other tangible rewards. See the section on reward systems.

Cooperative work should include (a) "class-building" activities to build class unity, (b) group- or team-building activities, and (c) partner activities. Having students work in pairs is an effective way to introduce content-packed activities, such as reading, writing, research, or math work, in a cooperative approach.

During the first month of school, teacher attention during cooperative activities should be focused on the procedures and interactions, *not on content.* Processing should occur during each cooperative activity to reflect on what was successful and to generalize the learning to other experiences. Processing questions for a group discussion might include the following:

◆ Why was your group successful (unsuccessful) in completing the task?
◆ Did you listen to your group?
◆ Did you develop any strategy for coming to a decision when people disagreed?
◆ How could you use that strategy on the playground or at home?

Class Meetings

Class meetings can be used for problem solving, topic discussions, determining class rules, deciding class functions, team-building activities, and positive interactions.

During these meetings, everyone sits in a circle, either on the floor or on chairs, so that all participants can have eye contact. Have the class practice getting into and out of the class-meeting circle (arrange desks, chairs, and so on) following the established procedures. Give students specific praise about what they did well each time. With practice, this should take one to two minutes.

The students may add items to the agenda as they deem necessary. The location for the agenda should be constant (a section of the chalkboard, a hanging clipboard). Keep minutes of the meeting to refer to. Teach students to make "I" statements, such as "I don't like so much noise during writer's workshop," instead of "John and Benito are talking too much." End with a compliment circle to close the meeting on a positive note. Model effective social skills.

Sample Procedure Chart for Class Meetings

1. Sit with bottoms on the floor (or all four legs of chair on floor).
2. Come empty-handed.
3. One person talks at a time; raise your hand to speak.
4. Focus on the speaker.
5. Participate.
6. You have the right to pass on a discussion.
7. Stay in the circle until the meeting is over.

1. Siéntate en el suelo (o con las cuatro patas de la silla en el suelo).
2. Deja todo en tu escritorio.
3. Levanta la mano para hablar; que hable una sola persona a la vez.
4. Fíjate en el orador.
5. Participa.
6. Tienes el derecho de no contribuir a la discusión.
7. Quédate en tu lugar en el círculo hasta que la reunión haya terminado.

TAILORING INSTRUCTION FOR ENGLISH LANGUAGE LEARNERS (ELL)

Students who learn English benefit from a variety of opportunities when natural language becomes connected to meaning. Meaning can be conveyed easily through pictures, actions, and explicit situations; for example, when handing someone a ball say, *Go play ball.*

The following examples demonstrate how teachers bring meaning to their lessons:

- ◆ Exaggerate gestures, facial expressions, and voice intonation.
- ◆ Limit sentence length and complexity; pause at the end of each sentence.
- ◆ Speak slowly, enunciate new vocabulary, pause after new words, and use synonyms.
- ◆ At the start of a lesson, define key words using familiar language.
- ◆ Clarify meaning; use pictures, props, motions, context clues, simpler words.
- ◆ Repeat, emphasize, and paraphrase key concepts.
- ◆ Summarize main ideas frequently.

Ask yourself: *"Does my lesson include a variety of strategies to help ELL students learn language and understand the lesson's context?"*

Questioning Strategies

Use questioning strategies often to ensure that students understand content and gain skill in using language. Questions should not be set up as a test but as an opportunity to practice language. Questioning strategies should be adapted to the students' language ability. Students with stronger English skills will need less support for their responses. Mixed groups require questioning strategies at every level, allowing opportunities for all to participate. Following are questions adapted for the stages used in English learning, starting with the earliest:

Hardly any English:

Ask questions your students can answer by moving their bodies. Model the expected behavior.
If your dress is red, stand up: Are you wearing a red dress? Model: Stand up.
Do you think the bears will find Goldilocks? Show a thumb up for yes, thumb down for no.

Beginning speech emerging:

Ask questions requiring short one-, two-, or three-word answers. Model the responses.
Where will Goldilocks go next: to the chair or to bed? (Point to illustrations as questions are asked).
Model sentence frames for students to practice and use in response to your questions:
What would you do with $100? Model several times: *If I had $100, I would buy a new bike,* or *if I had $100, I would buy a video game. What would you buy?*

Intermediate English skill level:

Build on student responses for modeling focus language patterns:
Mario says, I like soccer and football. Teacher expands, *Mario likes to play soccer, and he likes to play football. Sara, what do you like to play?*
Ask confirmation questions frequently. Before responding in the large group, have students pair and share.

More advanced level:

Ask students to repeat, paraphrase, or clarify what you or another student has said, enabling the sharing of information.
Ask yourself: *Have my questions allowed all students, whatever their English language proficiency, to participate in our discussion?*
The following strategies maximize student learning for all but are crucial to ELL students:

Build Lesson Backgrounds by Proceeding From Known to Unknown

During the first months of school, learn as much as possible about each student's family, home life, and community. Use concept maps to determine what students know about a topic by first placing the topic at the center of the page. Have students brainstorm their knowledge of the topic. Enter their responses. Feed new concepts into the map.

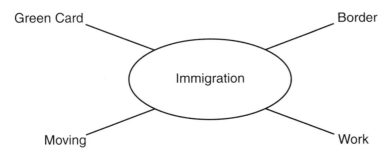

Ask yourself: *Does my lesson take students from WHAT they know to what I WANT them to know?*

Personalized Lessons

Students focus on lessons relating to their personal experiences—most specifically, themselves. Make a special effort to combine their world with each lesson:

- Draw examples from your students' experiences.
- Use pictures, books, and movies representing a variety of ethnic backgrounds.
- Use analogies relating new concepts to students' familiar experiences.

Ask yourself: *Has each student been personally involved in the lesson?*

Maximize Interaction

Students learn language when actively engaged in a lesson and more from peers than from their teacher. Provide opportunities for interaction within lessons. Working one-on-one with others and in small cooperative groups also fosters language development.

- Add songs, poems, and chants to reinforce the lesson's language.
- Before asking students to respond in a large group, provide opportunities for them to share with a buddy.
- Structure cooperative learning groups so all students have the opportunity to discuss things and share different roles within the group.

Ask yourself: *Have I provided a variety of ways for students to interact with material used in the lesson?*

Preview Lessons Orally

Previewing helps ELL students get beyond the mechanical difficulties of reading, enabling them to concentrate on lesson content. When previewing a lesson:

- Lead students sequentially through the chapter or lesson by outlining the primary concepts.
- Familiarize students with new vocabulary and idioms of the lesson.
- Connect language to illustrations.
- Discuss charts or graphs so that students learn to change graphic representation into language.
- Use the following strategies to combine student experience with your lesson: modeling, visuals, pictures, questioning, paraphrasing, restating, gesturing, and dramatic representation.

Ask yourself: *Has important content been conveyed and key vocabulary emphasized so that ELL students will understand the story when read aloud to them?*

Use Visuals, Graphic Organizers, and Hands-On Activities

Visuals, including those created by students, enhance their understanding of a concept:

- Graphic organizers help students arrange information. These may include charts, tables, diagrams, and graphs as well as concept maps for brainstorming/organizing information.
- Matrices, Venn diagrams, and other graphic organizing structures also help show relationships between information.
- Hands-on activities include experimentation, measuring, cutting, charting, weighing, and so on, and involve students more actively in the learning process. All students should share tools equally.

Ask yourself: *Have I chosen appropriate visuals and graphic organizers to help students envision the lesson content?*

Use of Effective Literature for English Language Learners

Quality literature and picture books are excellent tools for helping ELL students develop language and concepts. These suggestions assist in using books effectively with all students, including ELL learners.

How Do You Choose a Book?

♦ Read the entire book aloud to yourself.

♦ Choose one with illustrations that match the text.

♦ Use picture books with all age levels.

♦ Find books that contain clear examples of what you are attempting to teach.

♦ Make minimal use of idiomatic expressions.

♦ Find books that are large enough for students to see.

♦ Use books with simple sentence construction.

♦ Find books that can be read in five to ten minutes.

♦ Select books that can be read again and again.

♦ Look for repetitive or patterned language with opportunities for choral responses.

How to Introduce a Book for ELL Students That Determines Background Knowledge

♦ Set a purpose for reading, such as focusing on story structure (beginning, middle, and end) or language structure (e.g., past tense: *he walked to the store, he looked in the window*). Explain what they should do with this book. As you read the book aloud, model expected responses.

♦ Show the cover, read the title aloud, then ask, *What do you know about it?* Or give a brief preview, asking for predictions.

♦ Picture-walk. Flip through a few pages slowly, then ask, *What did you notice?*

♦ Preview idiomatic or difficult *content* words. Example: If the book is about a sorcerer, ask what students know about magic. As they share their schema related to magic, you can add the fact that one of the names for a magician is *sorcerer*.

♦ Think through what language/content you wish to use from the book. Your choice of activity helps students gain skills and knowledge from their experience with the book.

Focus on the Text's Language Structures and Vocabulary

♦ Imagine yourself as a second-language learner. Seek words or language structures that make the key point of the story difficult to understand. To get the meaning across, consider synonyms or gestures, intonation, hand movements, and use of illustrations.

♦ Create opportunities for helping students remember difficult vocabulary. Pictures can be drawn to illustrate nouns; motions may be used for verbs.

♦ Language games help in learning complex language constructions. Example: For the grammatical construction, "Would have done, could have done, should have done," make up chants/games for students to practice construction. *Who stole the cookies from the cookie jar?* is an example of a chanting game used to practice language and can be adapted for other language structures.

◆ Find opportunities for choral responses: You ask the question, model the response, and have all repeat the response together. Have students fill in the blanks for oral responses, hand motions, sound effects, or gestures (e.g., thumbs up).

Reading the Book

◆ Turn the book so students can see the pictures.

◆ Become an actor: Read slowly, but with expression; use your voice intonation to convey meaning. Track the print with your finger. Stop at key words and phrases and display the picture. Find opportunities for students to respond or interact with the text.

◆ Look at your students' faces frequently to determine if they are following you. Repeat questions to check who understands and who does not.

◆ Do not turn book sharing into a listening test. You are modeling reading while providing interactive opportunities for students to become involved in the book.

Ask yourself: *As I read this book aloud, are my students engaged in ways that will further their learning of language?*

STRATEGIES REGARDING BEHAVIOR

Promoting Good Behavior

If you have put all the previous information in place and still feel your management is not what it should be, we have some additional strategies you might employ:

◆ *Use "surprise" reinforcers.* Periodically, without warning, schedule a surprise for your class. Tell them the surprise is a direct result of their good behavior. For example, you might cancel a test, extend PE, have a special art project, or show a video.

◆ *Vary your lessons.* Often, disruptions occur because a task took too long. Determine the length of your students' attention span, and plan a change of task. Alternate activities that require large motor movements with those that are quieter.

◆ *Build relationships with your students.* Students are more willing to cooperate with people they like. Get to know them as individuals—use plenty of praise. Tell them what they do well. This is particularly effective with students with whom you are having difficulty. Force yourself to find out about those students so you can relate to them on a personal and positive level. Talk about topics they're interested in.

♦ *Be a good example.* Model the type of behavior you expect from your students. Model active listening, being prepared, thoughtfulness, and the like. Share your experiences with your students. Tell them how you have handled personal frustrations or how you enjoyed a book you just read.

♦ *Create an exciting curriculum.* Get the students involved in activities and discussions instead of passively listening and responding. This requires a lot of preparation and planning, but it can reduce disruptions.

Correcting Misbehavior

Occasionally, you will need to correct a misbehaving student. Here are some strategies to consider:

♦ *Look for simple solutions.* Make a list of specific inappropriate behaviors, then look for solutions. For example, if two students continue to talk, separate their desks. If students come late to class, use a stopwatch and deduct the time from their next break. Sometimes, students are able to brainstorm solutions to particular problems during class meetings.

♦ *Reinforce your procedures consistently.* Be specific about your behavioral expectations and post them. Use a reward system (see the next section). Have the consequences of disruptive behavior already thought out. Decide how you will record good and bad behavior (e.g., individually, by tables, or whole class, using tallies, stars, or stickers). Explain your plan to your students and follow through the first time a student misbehaves.

♦ *Reward good behavior.* Verbally praise the specific behavior you want to reinforce. For instance, "Ruth is following directions," or "Fred cleaned up his desk and is ready to listen," is more specific than "I like the way Ruth is helping," or "Good job, Fred." Catch the students being good, especially those who misbehave most.

♦ *Write behavior contracts.* If a certain student constantly disrupts the class, write a contract with him or her that is specific and appropriate to the misbehavior. The contract should include (a) the desired behavior (e.g., raising hand before talking), (b) how often the behavior must occur (e.g., 100 percent of the time), (c) the reinforcer (e.g., a ten-minute break in class each day), and (d) the term of the contract (e.g., a week or less). Note that this contract should be developed with the student, especially the reinforcer.

♦ *Report to parents and guardians.* These reports are most effective if they are positive. Call the parents and tell them how well their child is doing or behaving in class. If after you've tried a contract with no change in student behavior, enlist parent/caregiver support. Often, parents can help determine reinforcers (e.g., extra TV time, special family event) or consequences (e.g., no skateboarding, no TV).

Remember: A positive classroom environment requires consistency, modeling, and practice. It does not happen magically.

Reward Systems

There are a variety of ways you may choose to reward your students to reinforce their following of procedures. Reward systems are used initially to motivate students to try to succeed at a new behavior. The system is kept in place until mastery of the desired behavior has occurred, and then it is phased out. Edible rewards (popcorn, raisins), tangible rewards (stickers, prizes), and tokens (points, tickets) are all low-level reinforcers. Our goal in using reward systems is to develop internal motivation in our students. Vary the rewards over time. Following are some ideas:

♦ *The marble jar.* The class earns marbles for good behavior, and these are displayed in a jar. When the jar is filled, the class has earned a special privilege, such as a party or the chance to watch a video. Start with a small jar.

♦ *Secret words.* The teacher determines a positive consequence for the class and a secret word to be spelled. When the class earns a letter for good behavior, it is put on the bulletin board. When the word is spelled, the class receives the consequence (e.g., popcorn, free play, video, picnic, party).

♦ *Grab bags.* Individuals earn points through academic work or behavior. A certain number of points lets them pick an object or certificate (e.g., the chance to be a team leader or special monitor, extra free time, a free homework pass).

♦ *Rent classroom valuables.* Through appropriate behavior, students can rent classroom objects, such as puzzles, games, special books, or toys, for overnight or weekend use.

♦ *Raffle or auction.* Students earn raffle tickets for appropriate behavior. After a period of time, students bring objects from home, with their parents' permission, and hold a raffle.

♦ *Preferred activity time.* Give the whole class unconditional time for academically related games (fifteen to twenty minutes for Around the World, Jeopardy, Spelling or Math Baseball, or the like). The time can be taken away from the whole class for misbehavior or from individuals who don't finish work or constantly disrupt.

DAILY ONGOING ACTIVITIES

Silent Reading

Set clear procedures for silent reading (for K–1, this should be called *quiet reading,* and students should be allowed to share and converse quietly about their books). Have students choose the books they will read before going to recess or lunch, and have them waiting on their desks when they come in, or have boxes of books at each table. If a student chooses short, simple books, have two or three on the desk so he or she will not have to get up. In lower grades, start silent reading in short intervals, increasing the time each day to twenty to thirty minutes.

During the first few weeks, use this opportunity to assess students. Walk around and note names of books and page numbers each day to see if students are moving through their books. Ask students to read quietly to you from their books and ask some simple questions to determine their levels of understanding. Don't verbalize any judgments to them about books being too hard or too easy. During silent reading, they may read whatever they want. Use the information you gather to suggest books that they may enjoy at the library or at other times in class. Work toward being able to sit down and read a book yourself during silent reading time. This makes a strong statement to students.

Sample Procedure Chart for Silent Reading

1. Have your books ready. 2. Come in silently and get your book. 3. Remain in your seat. 4. Read silently. 5. Read the entire time. 6. When silent reading is over, you may share something you enjoyed.
1. Tengan listos sus libros. 2. Entren calladitos y tomen sus libros. 3. Manténganse en sus asientos. 4. Lean en silencio. 5. Lean durante todo el tiempo. 6. Cuando se termine la lectura personal pueden compartir algo que les gustó.

Read-Alouds

Daily exposure to quality literature increases the desire to read independently and models many reading skills. Schedule ten to fifteen minutes for primary grades and twenty to thirty minutes for older students. In bilingual classes, don't be afraid to read stories in students' second language; think in terms of emerging comprehension. Give visual cues and use strategies such as alternate day and preview-review. (See the section on ELL strategies on page 57).

Sometimes, discuss the story with the class; predict action, clarify vocabulary in context, analyze the plot, and visualize the setting. Don't overdo the discussion—remember that your main purpose is for them to enjoy the author's work. Don't analyze every story.

Preview the book before beginning with the class. Look for appropriateness to grade level (length of passages, vocabulary, interest), and familiarize yourself with characters and points to be highlighted.

When creating procedures for read-aloud time, think about the following questions:

- Where will the students sit?
- May they draw or write, or do you want them looking at you?
- May they get up and sharpen pencils, get a drink of water, or the like?

The following chart of sample procedures assumes that you will allow the children to draw while they listen to you read.

Sample Procedure Chart for Read-Aloud

1. Get all materials for drawing before reading begins.
2. Stay seated.
3. Listen silently.
4. Clean up.
1. Agara Recojen todas las materias de dibujar antes de que la maestra comienza a leer.
2. Manténte sentado.
3. Escucha en silencio.
4. Recoge todo.

Journals

Journals may be created by stapling several sheets of paper into a construction paper folder. For beginning writers, a large drawing space with a few lines underneath is great. By third or fourth grade, the drawing space can be eliminated. Journals are places for students to write their thoughts on a daily basis, with content being important, not mechanics. Creative spelling should be encouraged by not spelling for students. Journals may be interactive; that is, the teacher may write back to the students.

Journal writing, like any activity, must be modeled. A teacher can do this by writing right alongside students. Reading from personal journals, as well as reading from journals of historians, writers, and others, are good models for students. You can also demonstrate the process on an overhead projector to show that journal writing is just writing down thoughts.

Sample Procedure Chart for Journals

1. Write for ten minutes silently.
2. Write about anything you like or choose a topic from the board.
3. Don't worry about punctuation.
4. Invent your own spelling.
5. Stay in your seat.

1. Escribe en silencio durante diez minutos.
2. Escribe sobre cualquier cosa o escoge un tema del pizarrón.
3. No te preocupes por la puntuación.
4. Inventa cómo deletrear las palabras.
5. Quédate en tu asiento.

Figure 3.5   Calendar Ideas

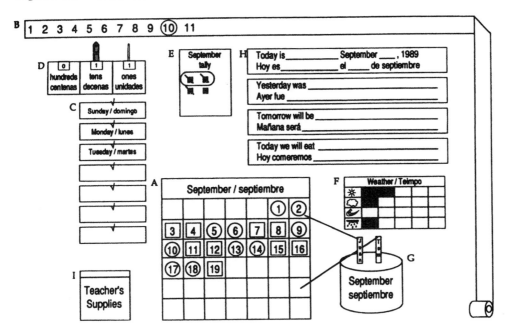

Literature Logs

Literature logs are similar to journals, but rather than writing on a particular topic, students respond to literature. They may respond to the read-aloud or to their own silent reading. Their logs may reflect class discussions or just their own private reactions.

Calendar, K–2

The purpose of doing a calendar routine is to provide real-life math experiences for your students. It usually requires ten to twenty minutes per day. As students learn the procedures, provide for some rotation so each student can be the leader. Choosing a "captain" or "helper" to help you each day allows you to become the facilitator.

Figure 3.5 illustrates various ideas for the calendar. Choose the ones you feel are appropriate to your grade level and in which you can maintain interest. Keep your calendar time simple, flexible, and interesting. As you add new items to the calendar, be sure you model them.

Setting up the calendar takes some time at the beginning of the year, but most parts will stay up all year, with just a few monthly changes needed. Specific things you will need for each part of the calendar bulletin board follow. The letters correspond to the illustrations in Figure 3.5:

A: *Month pattern grid calendar.* The month calendar grid is displayed with only the name of the month and the days of the week at the beginning of a month. The grid should contain squares of about 3 by 3 inches. Each day, add the marker that corresponds to the date. You need to make daily markers to fit the grid squares based on a pattern (e.g., shapes, seasonal cutouts, color). Keep the daily markers in the teacher supply container (see the following explanation of I). Use this to reinforce the date, the pattern, and the days of the week.

B: *Days-of-school graph.* Use adding-machine tape with a string tied through the roll so it can be pinned to the wall. Record with black each day you are in school, marking the 10s in a red pen and circling them. This graph can be used for daily rote counting activities as well as development of the understanding of the pattern of the base-10 number system.

C: *Days of the week.* Make 3-inch by 8-inch strips of tagboard with the days of the week written on them. Punch a hole in the center of each card so it can be hung from a pin and easily turned over. Turn over only those days that have already passed. This activity is done in conjunction with a days-of-the-week song (see Chapter 6). Talk about how many days have gone by in a week and how many are yet to come. Responses can be written in number sentence form (e.g., $3 + 4 = 7$).

D: *Number line straw box.* Use three half-gallon milk cartons cut down to 4 inches high. Cover these with Con-Tact paper (in three different colors, if you want to make the place value more visual). Label the boxes "ones," "tens," and "hundreds." Attach a set of flip numerals to each carton. The straw count will match the days of school graph. Add one straw each day, bundling the tens as they occur. Use this to count by tens and ones with your students.

E: *Monthly tally.* Use a 9-inch by 12-inch piece of newsprint or a small chalkboard nailed to your bulletin board. Make a tally mark for each day of the month, circling the tens. The tally count corresponds to the monthly calendar. Count the tally marks each day, using the tens or fives as a starting point. Ask prediction questions, such as "How many more days until we can circle a 10 again? A group of 5?"

F: *Weather graph.* Make a grid with pictures for sunny, cloudy, rainy, etc. on the left side and at least fifteen squares across. Each day, have the captain or leader determine the weather outside and color a square next to the appropriate type of weather. At the end of the month, a total tally can be made. Display the graphs of each month and use them for an analysis of how the weather changes over the year.

G: *Birthday graph.* Before the beginning of school, prepare a birthday cake or similar representation for each month of the school year. If you use a birthday cake, have each student write (or you write) his or her birthday on a candle. After discussing the birthday graph, use the twelve cakes and candles for a permanent bulletin board display. Put the "cake of the month" on the calendar bulletin board, with the appropriate students' candles, and use yarn or roving to indicate where each birthday falls on the monthly calendar.

H: *Date or menu strips.* Use sentence strip tagboard to make the sentences shown in Figure 3.5. Make day-of-the-week cards to fit the blanks, as well as month and numeral cards to fit the blank spaces. Also, make cards for the main-dish items on your school menu. The captain can find these cards, read the menu, and select the appropriate card, then read the completed sentences or choose someone to read the sentences when the cards have been placed.

I: *Teacher supplies.* Use a Ziploc bag or small box stapled to the bulletin board to store the supplies you will need to do the calendar: black and red wide felt-tip pens, the date markers for the monthly calendar, the day-of-the-week cards for the date strips, extra pins, and so on.

The First Two Weeks of School . . . A Detailed Account

This chapter provides detailed instructions to get you through the first two weeks of school. A sample schedule is provided that you may adapt to meet your needs. This chapter helps you create routines that train students how to work independently, allowing you, the teacher, to focus on smaller group, teacher-directed instruction while the rest of the class works independently. This training is crucial to the success of your classroom for the entire year. This approach allows you to differentiate instruction to meet the needs of English learners while providing rigorous academic content for all students. This two-week period is the time in which you set your routines for the year in all subject areas.

OVERVIEW OF THE FIRST TWO WEEKS OF SCHOOL FOR KINDERGARTEN AND FIRST GRADE

Your goal for the first day and first weeks will be to build a community where learning takes place and where all (parents, children, teachers) feel valued, respected, and safe. This is a big responsibility, and the task begins the first minute of the first day of school.

Your first day as a kindergarten or first-grade teacher can be challenging. Kindergarten students may be very unsure of themselves. First graders might have to experience a longer day along with other new and unfamiliar school routines. Parents often accompany young children on the first day. Handling both the children's insecurities and their parents' concerns can be a daunting task. On the first day, you may invite parents to attend for a specific period of time. Gently but firmly adhere to this rule. Be sure to acknowledge parents' interest in their children's education; also, communicate that their participation will be valued and needed. But on the first day, you need time to bond with your students without their parents.

Remember that you will be teaching routines, procedures, and dynamics of your ideal environment. Also remember that on the first day, and in the first weeks, your students should be aware of and identify with your vision in order to become valued members of the learning community. Careful planning will see you through. This section contains detailed sample schedules and lesson plans. Here are some tips:

- ♦ On the first day, set up tables with easy puzzles and games, paper and crayons, books, and so on. (Don't include activities requiring major cleanup—your students have not yet mastered those tasks.)

- ♦ Greet children and parents at the door. Start learning names immediately. Remind parents that at your signal (bell, chime, etc.), they should help their children clean up and proceed to the group meeting area.

- ♦ Ask children to store backpacks, sweaters, and so forth in any available cubby. Creating names for their cubbies will follow later as a small-group activity.

- ♦ In kindergarten, arrange to have your coteacher work with you all day, if possible. Reciprocate during her or his session.

- ♦ On the first day, try to schedule aide or helper time during the beginning and end of day, at a minimum. In kindergarten, having another adult assist you all day is optimal.

- ♦ Arrange your schedule to include whole-group meetings that last no longer than fifteen or twenty minutes. Young children tire more easily while sitting than when active. If movement activities are included, extend the time to thirty minutes.

- ♦ Be prepared with a variety of activities that focus on building your vision of a classroom community.

◆ Be prepared to have patience! Activities may take longer the first days.

Note: Locate at your school site or purchase one of the titles listed in the Resources section under "Literacy." To fully understand how to implement the strategies outlined in this chapter, you will need more information than is provided in this book. We are simply getting you started.

FIRST TWO WEEKS OF SCHOOL—KINDERGARTEN

Day 1

Welcome Parents and Children: 20–30 Minutes

Preparation:

◆ Have name tags ready on a table.

◆ Have other tables or areas set up in the room with simple activities (e.g., simple puzzles, Play-Doh, books, paper and crayons, etc.).

◆ Your class list should include names, addresses, bus routes and stops, and so on—*all* information you have gathered.

Greet parents and children as they arrive. Using your class list, ask parents to review their child's pertinent information. Make required changes immediately. Ask parents to locate their child's name tag on the table and then engage in an activity with their child at another table. If possible, have an adult (aide, coteacher) supervise the tables, keeping parents and children busy.

Hint: Prepare STOP signs to hang in front of any activity that is not open—a visual reminder to both parents and children of your off-limits areas.

After twenty to thirty minutes, make your Freeze-and-Listen signal. Model how you wish children, parents to respond. Be sure other adults respond as well. This may take time—even with the help and cooperation of all adults—to accomplish this transition. Do not give up! Practice until all students have stopped and are looking at you. Praise, praise, praise those who are frozen. Say something such as, "It's time to clean up and come to the meeting area. Everyone, please help to clean up your area. Parents, please help the children clean up; come and sit at our meeting area, then you may leave. We'll see you at the end of the day." You might sing a cleanup song to signal the start of cleanup.

Note: Expect some students to cry and be upset when parents are asked to leave. Try not to get upset—your demeanor and body language should convey to the child (and caregivers) that the child will be fine. When trying to conduct your normal routine, it can be disconcerting to have a child wailing in the background, but do proceed! Ask other adults to help console the crying child or children. Try these strategies:

- Gently pry him or her from the parent's grasp; move child to Circle Area with the other students.

- Assure parents that the child will be fine and the situation will improve if they leave. Have them leave!

- Ask another adult to sit with the child at the circle and to gently and quietly console the child. If the child is wailing loudly, have adult and child move outside the circle. When crying has lessened to a tolerable noise level, have the adult bring the child back to the circle.

- Have the child work with his or her small group. Always use words that mean *exactly* what is happening and what to expect but also ensure that he or she *will* become part of your class routine.

- For the first day, move the child through class routines. If another adult is assisting you, instruct that person to try to engage the child in whatever activity he or she should be doing at the time. Instruct the adult to move away when the child has become integrated.

- Follow these guidelines if crying recurs. If the child is removed from class, you will be in jeopardy. Invite an older sibling to assist by conveying the message, "If you cry, you will be segregated from class routines." Your goal is to integrate the child into the class and to demonstrate that the classroom is a safe and fun place.

- Inconsolable, long-term criers (continuing for more than one week) might need special intervention. Parents should be contacted and a conference arranged for all to strategize. You might also contact your principal, resource teachers, or special education personnel to help devise a plan.

Whole-Group Opening: 20 Minutes

Preparation:

- Have available a list of fingerplays and songs to sing. Write these down—you will be surprised how quickly you can forget!

- Have on hand several simple books to read. *Spot* and *Clifford* are good choices.

- Use a puppet for introductions

Once most of the children have your attention, start a fingerplay. *Do it*, without trying to *teach it* (see Chapter 6). Sing and chant until all have arrived at the meeting area. Say goodbye to parents; thank them for attending. Reassure children that they will see their families soon.

Introductions:

♦ Introduce all adults in the room. While saying the person's name, write it on chalkboard or chart paper, slowly repeating the name as you write it. Teach students to say, "Hello, Mrs. Smith."

♦ Introduce your puppet. (Choose a name starting with a letter not represented by your students' names.) Announce that "Beto" is everyone's friend and wants to learn each student's name. Walk up to each child in turn, saying: "Hi, I'm Beto. What's your name?" When the child responds, say: "Hello, Sandi" (for the puppet). Whenever a child is too shy or nervous to respond, simply say, "Hello, José," and proceed to the next student.

♦ Sing another song.

♦ Follow with a bathroom tour—usually necessary by this time. For this task, another adult's help will be needed. Dismiss students individually to line up—girls first, then boys. Discuss how they should stand, one behind the other, hands by sides. Praise those who comply by stating exactly what they are doing correctly: "María has her hands by her sides and is standing right behind Jessica."

During the bathroom tour, introduce and reinforce these points:

♦ How to use toilet paper

♦ How to flush

♦ How to wash hands

♦ Where to throw trash

Allow those who need to use the bathroom to do so. Return to class. If one group returns early, the adult in charge can start reading any available book.

Small-Group Directed Activities: 60 Minutes

An appropriate focus of the first week's small-group activities is to introduce and train students to work with all materials, games, and center areas of your classroom. (See Chapter 1, "A Guide to Planning and Creating the Environment," for suggestions on setting up your room.) Kindergarten provides a time block for students to freely explore their environment and make self-selected choices. For them to make good choices and work independently, they must learn the "dos and don'ts" for each activity.

Remember: Never assume that they will understand or use materials appropriately without an introduction. Remember this each time you introduce something new to the environment!

Preparation:

♦ Prepare a list of all areas, centers, and activities already set up.

- ◆ Consider what students must know before using the materials, cleaning up appropriately, and working together at the center.
- ◆ Plan, in order, which centers will be introduced first, second, and third.

Divide class into as many groups as there are adults to supervise. (See Chapter 1 for color-coding name tags so you can create initial student groups). The optimal number is three adults. Plan to do three rotations of twenty minutes each for each of the first three or four days, depending on the number of activities you will introduce. The sample plan shown in Table 4.1 uses three adults.

Table 4.1   Small-Group Directed Activities

	Group 1	**Group 2**	**Group 3**
Day 1, rotation 1	Play-Doh Small playhouse Farm	Writing center	Playground toys and structure (done outside)
Day 1, rotation 2	Playground toys and structure (done outside)	Play Doh Small playhouse Farm	Writing center
Day 1, rotation 3	Writing center	Playground toys and structure (done outside)	Play-Doh Small playhouse Farm
Day 2, rotation 1	Toy shelf	Dramatic play Lego®	Blocks
Day 2, rotation 2	Blocks	Toy shelf	Dramatic play Lego®
Day 2, rotation 3	Dramatic play Lego®	Blocks	Toy shelf
Day 3, rotation 1	Listening center Sand table	Math manipulatives	Art center: easels and watercolors
Day 3, rotation 2	Art center: easels and watercolors	Listening center Sand table	Math manipulatives
Day 3, rotation 3	Math manipulatives	Art center: easels and watercolors	Listening center Sand table

Each adult oversees one activity and introduces the following information to each successive group:

- ◆ Purpose of the center: "At the Listening Center, we will listen to stories, using earphones."

♦ The number of children who may be at the center and what they should do in order to be there: "There are just enough places for four people to use the earphones at the Listening Center." Some centers are easily defined by the number of seats; others may need "entry tickets," such as clip-ons, tags, or necklaces to clearly identify who is permitted at any given time.

♦ How materials and equipment will be used: Be sure to model these instructions. For example, demonstrate how to insert a cassette into a tape recorder, then ask one or two children to model doing it. Have student volunteers model also.

● Behavior that isn't permitted: Demonstrate a negative behavior, such as randomly pushing the buttons on the tape recorder. Ask children to explain why it is not OK to do that.

This introduction should take seven to ten minutes, then students can work at the center(s).

Remember: Don't introduce ten students to the Listening Center when only four can participate. Instead, introduce the Center together with the Blocks Area, where six children can participate.

After fifteen to eighteen minutes, make your Freeze-and-Listen signal. Teachers at each center supervise cleanup, then line up their students. At your signal, groups rotate. A rotation schedule of twenty-minute groups should be used only during the first few days.

Once routines and procedures are established for these ongoing activities, small-group time can develop into direct instruction. Plan at least thirty minutes for each group. If you decide on two daily rotations, small-group time extends to sixty minutes. We suggest a forty-five-minute group without rotations. After small-group time, students gather at your meeting area to prepare for outdoor play.

Remember:

♦ Reinforce what students have learned during small-group time about rules and procedures for the playground area.

♦ Snack time may be included during this time period. Introduce and model procedures for eating areas: how to dispose of trash, where lunch boxes should be left, and so on.

♦ Introduce your signal designating the end of recess. Model how and where students should line up, and so on.

Outdoor Play and Snack: 15–20 Minutes

In kindergarten, it is usual for cooperating teachers to trade supervision of outdoor play, so others have time for breaks and to set up future activities. Try to make this happen.

Whole-Group Circle: 15 Minutes

Use fingerplays to settle your students. Repetition of those done earlier is a good idea. Use the calendar routine (see Chapter 3, "Routines and Procedures"). On the first day, you may model this activity rather than using a student helper.

Read a story. Continue on, and you will understand why this is not as simple as it sounds! Reading aloud should occur at least three times a day and should be an enjoyable community-building experience. Use two types of reading-aloud material: (a) small-format books and (b) large books, charts, or other enlarged text.

♦ Small-format books—stories, magazines, and picture books—provide shared reading experiences showing why and how we read. Books chosen to enhance themes, learn new ideas, and share classic tales challenge students to be good listeners and to understand story structure and expository texts.

♦ Enlarged print in big books, charts, and so on, aids in teaching students how to read. Choose resource books from those listed in the Resource section. These will guide you in becoming a strategic reading teacher during shared-reading experiences.

Introduce *your* routine for reading aloud: Should students sit in front of you? Can they lie down? Be sure that all can see the book and become part of the group experience. Explain the procedure, model it, then have one or two volunteers do the same. Last, have students demonstrate that they know the procedure by inviting them to follow it. Praise specifically. Redirect those who should try again by being clear, consistent, and firm. Do not proceed until all have shown that they understand the procedure.

Preparation for a read-aloud session:

♦ Choose a book that will interest your students.

♦ Read the book in advance; consider how you can make the story come alive by using different voices for each character, pointing out something in the illustrations, encouraging children to join in on the repetitive parts.

♦ Plan teaching points and questions to be asked. Note ideas and questions on Post-it notes; place these in the book as reminders.

Tour the School: 20 Minutes

Take a school tour. Again, it is best to divide students into two or more groups to facilitate learning to walk in line and to go in and out of places easily. If another adult is available, plan two different routes so each group will tour independently. Tours should include the office, library, cafeteria, large playground, and bathrooms outside the kindergarten room—all places unique to your school. Alert appropriate personnel to the approximate time of your tour; ask that they be prepared to briefly introduce themselves and their jobs.

Closing: 20 Minutes

You've almost made it! Collect name tags. Recap the day. Students might share something they liked or learned today, an adult noting their ideas on chart paper. You might teach a goodbye song or read another story. Whatever your choice, end the day calmly and in anticipation of tomorrow's activities.

During the first weeks, remember to prepare whatever is needed to ensure your students' safe arrival home:

- ◆ Allow time to affix bus tags.
- ◆ Know which students have older siblings who will collect them.
- ◆ Arrive at the bus-loading zone with ample time to spare.
- ◆ Keep your class list of student information with you at all times.
- ◆ Arrange a "waiting spot" for parents who will pick up their children.

What's Next?

One key to a smoothly running classroom is that children *know* what to expect. After the first day, your challenge will be to establish schedules with clear routines for each time block. This might be accomplished the first day, but remember, children must practice and internalize these routines over time.

During the first two weeks, continue to reinforce all procedures and routines. Be explicit as to *why* routine is important:

"We need to sit and listen so we can enjoy the story. Juan, come and show us how to get ready to listen to this story. Great! Did everyone see how Juan stood up and walked to our story place? Then he sat down and looked at the book. Raise your hand if you think you can do that, too. OK, come on!"

You might need to model and review often before routines are established. The key to a successful year is based on the climate established through clear, frequent, and consistent routines. Practice with students until you are successful.

The following sample schedule will lead you through the next two weeks. Base your schedule on when help is available, the playground schedule—any details unique to your school.

Sample Kindergarten Schedule

30 minutes:	Opening Circle
45–60 minutes:	Small-group instruction
15–20 minutes:	Snack/recess
20 minutes:	Circle Time/English language development
50 minutes:	Exploration Time (pull a small group for targeted instruction)
20 minutes:	Closing Circle

Established Routines for Opening Circle

(These can be done in any order.)

Choosing a Helper for the Day:

- Write each student's name on a three-by-five-inch card. Hole punch one corner, place cards in alphabetical order on a ring.
- Using the first child as your helper, flip to the next name on the following day, and so forth.

Bonus: Students learn alphabetical order easily when following this method.

- When this method is first introduced, show students that all names are included in the pack. Assure them that they all will get a turn.
- Tasks for Helper of the Day: Lead calendar routine (see Monthly Calendar Lesson in Chapter 5), take roll sheet to the office, serve as line leader, excuse students to line up, and so on. (This system eliminates the need for a jobs chart.)

Taking roll:

- Prepare a pocket chart, placing a Yes/Sí and No card in the top pocket.
- Write each child's name on a tagboard strip.
- Daily, hold up each student's name card. Encourage the class to read that name with you.
- As you read, use your finger for tracking beneath the letters.
- Following that, ask student to come forward and get her or his card, placing it under Yes/Sí to indicate that she or he is present. For those absent, the Helper places the card under No.
- Optional: Count how many children are present or absent.
- Mark the roll sheet; send it to the office with the Helper and a friend. (Have an adult accompany them the first few times to make sure they know the route.)
- Later, you can enliven this routine: Pose a yes-or-no question. Have students use their roll card to answer on the pocket chart: "Do you have a brother?" or "Do you like to play soccer?" Students may also create a simple bar graph in response to choices: "What group are you in?"

Calendar Routine:

- See Chapter 3 for a detailed explanation and Chapter 5 for sample calendar grids.

Note: Choose only those pieces of the calendar routine that students need and can complete. Others can be added during the year.

Incorporate These Activities During Any Circle Time

Music/Movement:

♦ Songs, poems, and chants should become a regular part of your day.

♦ Singing and chanting together is a wonderful community builder, a way to relax, focus, and reenergize.

♦ Using enlarged charts of known songs, poems, and rhymes is fundamental to the teaching of reading. (Refer to your resource book.)

Shared Writing:

♦ Daily, spend time writing before the students on chart paper. This enables them to see how writing works. As you write, vocalize words, then sounds.

♦ Writing can be used for the *Morning Message,* to record students' ideas, or to pose a question during roll call.

♦ Don't drag this out; this should not take more than five minutes.

♦ During the writing, speak explicitly about how one writes: left to right, leaving spaces between words, letters and sounds, and so forth.

Reading Aloud or Shared Reading:

♦ Continue to reinforce and model the routine explained in Day 1.

Demonstrations, Discussions, Whole-Group Lessons:

♦ Model, introduce, and present any new or available activity.

♦ Show and discuss objects that relate your teaching to real life such as photos, clothing from another era, or topics of interest related to your theme.

♦ Conduct whole-class exploration of a math, science, or literacy concept.

Continuing What You've Begun:

Take a look at Table 4.2, which graphs sample activities for the rest of the first week.

The activities listed in Table 4.2 cannot all be accomplished in twenty–thirty minutes, so plan them throughout the day. Timing should be gauged by your students' attention and interest. Pacing is very important. If students are not attending, they will not learn.

Table 4.2   Opening Circle: The Next Four Days

	Day 2	**Day 3**	**Day 4**	**Day 5**
Music	Sing a Hello song. Revisit songs from Day 1.	Same	Teach "The Wheels on the Bus".	Same
Helper	Next name	Next name	Next name	Next name
Roll	Read names. Place by Yes/No.	Same	Read names. Place by how they come and go from school (e.g., icons for bus, car, walk).	Read names. Each child places name card on pocket chart under the symbol for her or his group.
Calendar routine	Model with Helper.	Model with Helper.	Helper does alone with your support.	Helper does alone with your support.
Shared writing	None here	None here	Write bus safety rules (e.g., "Sit in your seat." or "Talk softly.").	Write before roll call, "What is your group? En qué grupo estás?"
Read aloud	After introducing discipline system, read a book about a first day at school.	Read a Clifford book. Talk about how Clifford is a friend.	Read/sing a book with "The Wheels on the Bus/Las Ruedas del Bus." Discuss children's experiences with buses.	Read *The Little Red Hen/La Gallinita Roja.* Discuss being helpful in the classroom.
Demonstration	Introduce your discipline system. Model and role-play with children. Be liberal in your positive rewards all day and all week.	Revisit and role-play problems you have spotted in any class routine. Connect to your discussion of friendship from read-aloud time.	Role-play safe conduct on a bus.	Revisit and role-play problems spotted in any class routine. Connect discussion to read-aloud time (e.g., "How is the like (unlike) what the little red hen did?").

Now, it is your turn. Many of these routines are in place. Using Table 4.3, plug in the Circle Time activities you wish to teach. Check curriculum guides for literacy, math, and English language development (ELD). What are good choices for Days 7 through 9?

Table 4.3   Planning Days 6 Through 9

	Day 6	**Day 7**	**Day 8**	**Day 9**
Music	Teach "The More We Get Together."			
Helper	Next name			
Roll	Same See Shared Writing for prompt.			
Calendar routine	Same			
Shared writing	Write: "Which character would you like to be in *The Little Red Hen?*"			
Read aloud	Retell *The Little Red Hen* with simple props.			
Demonstration	Revisit procedures that are not in place; model and role-play.			

Small-Group Instruction: 45 Minutes

Once children have been introduced and trained to use various permanent areas in your room, small-group instruction becomes more targeted. If you follow the Small-Group Directed Activities plan that was outlined in Table 4.1, you can start permanent small-group instruction on Day 4.

A detailed plan for Days 4 through 9, shown in Table 4.4, is based on three adults for group instruction. If less are available, one student group might work at independent centers (Writing, Listening, Alphabet, or Library Centers) during small-group instructional time. If an Independent Group is planned, include these centers during training time so students learn to work independently. Arrange for an older student helper to supervise the Independent Group.

This plan uses a forty-five-minute group time without rotations. Each group remains with the group teacher for that time period. Students perform different activities each day; therefore, three days are needed for all to proceed through each center.

Table 4.4   Small-Group Activities: Days 4 Through 9

	Days 4 Through 6	**Days 7 Through 9**
Literacy	**Cut-and-Paste Bus**	**Class Book**
	Materials and preparation Precut 3" x 5" yellow rectangles, 1 per child 9" x 12" white construction paper, 1 per child Precut 2" black squares Crayons and pencils Scissors	**Materials and preparation** A short book about school: (e.g., *Things I Like/Cosas que me gusta* by Anthony Browne; *I am Six/Tengno seis años* by Ann Morris) Chart paper and pen Duplicated sheet with "At school, I like to___/En la escuela me gusta___" written at the bottom; 1 per child. Crayons Pencils
	Procedure Review "The Wheels on the Bus." Explain that students will make their own pictures of a bus. Discuss their experiences riding on buses. Model how to draw windows, door, and faces in a window on a yellow rectangle, then paste rectangle in the center of the white paper. Model writing your name on the back of the white paper. (*Note*: Do not write names for students.) Allow them to get their name cards from the Roll and then copy their names to the best of their abilities. Model how to draw circles on black paper. Cut them out and paste them on the yellow rectangle as wheels. Model how to draw a road and background on the white paper. Pass out supplies to children. Pass out yellow rectangles and crayons. Pass out additional materials as needed by individuals. Have each student share with the group.	**Procedure** Read and discuss the book. Write the sentence starter on chart paper in front of the children. Have each child share something he or she likes to do at school. Write each idea on the chart. Read each child's idea, starting with the sentence starter. (e.g., Alicia said, "At school I like to paint.") Track the print as you read. Model how to write your name, then fill in the blank on the duplicated sheet, and draw a picture. In this demonstration, include how to use materials and how to clean up. Assist students as needed. Some children will be able to write independently; some will need your help. Collect all pages and keep. Make a simple book cover entitled, At School, We Like to . . . by____. Collate all student pages. During Circle Time on Day 10, read the book to the students, have them sign their names as authors, add page numbers, and so on.

(Continued)

Table 4.4 (Continued)

Math	Exploration of Math Manipulatives	Take-home Calendar
	Materials and preparation Have available the tubs of the math manipulatives presented during Days 1 through 3. **Procedure** Review characteristics of each manipulative (e.g., What do you notice about____?) Review how to use each manipulative. Allow children to choose which manipulative to work with. Notice what they do with the manipulative. Ask questions of individuals regarding colors, shapes, counting, and so on to get an idea of who knows what.	**Materials and preparation** Duplicate the calendar grid found in Chapter 5 (write in month, year, and dates from 11 on, before duplicating). Have ready 1 per child plus extras for teacher-modeling. Staple grid onto a 12" x 18" piece of construction paper; fold in half so students can first work on the calendar portion, then the art. Select an art activity to decorate top portion of the calendar (something simple, such as a self-portrait). Number chart Pencils **Procedure** Pass out calendars. Ask what students notice. Discuss what they know about calendars. Provide some simple information. Read month and year together. See Chapter 5 for monthly calendar procedures.
Extension	Cubby names	Collage names
	Materials and preparation Prelabel each cubby with a student's name. Write name on a piece of masking tape. Cubbies should be labeled in ABC order. Have construction paper cut to fit inside cubby. Write students' names in large letters on paper. Any collage items (stickers, cut-outs, magazines, spangles, etc.) Glue **Procedure** Show the name of each child in group. Assess who recognizes own name and reads other's names. Show collage items. Discuss how they might be used to decorate names. Have students decorate. As each one finishes, take him or her to the prelabeled cubby; attach decorated name.	**Materials and preparation** Cut 4" x 12" pieces from a variety of colored construction paper, 1 per child. Write child's name in very large, spaced-out lettering. Beans, colored macaroni, any small 3D objects available. Glue **Procedure** Show the name of each child to the group. Again, assess what they know or have learned about each other's and their own names. Introduce the materials available to decorate their names. Model how you will apply glue on one letter of their names, then they carefully put materials on that line of glue. Apply a line of glue on each child's first letter. Monitor and repeat with each additional letter.

Have materials needed for each activity in a tub or box at the table. The content of the activities is not as important as reinforcing and practicing what it means to work in a small group. Keep activities simple. All adults must reinforce how students should sit, listen, work together, and pass out and use supplies, such as glue, paper, and so on. Those who finish early may read from the tub of books at each table.

The following sample rotation schedule includes three groups: Red, Yellow, and Blue:

	Days 4 and 7	*Days 5 and 8*	*Days 6 and 9*
Literacy	Blue	Red	Yellow
Math	Yellow	Blue	Red
Extension or Independent	Red	Yellow	Blue

Following group time, make your Freeze-and-Listen signal. Have the class stop and freeze. Be clear and consistent about this expectation. Ask adults and children to clean their areas, then proceed to the whole-group meeting area.

Outdoor Play, Snack: 15–20 Minutes

Reinforce expected behavior before leaving the classroom. Remind students to use the bathroom, get a drink of water, exercise, and have fun. If you have a break, set up Exploration activities.

Exploration: 45–60 Minutes

Remember small-group instruction for Days 1 and 2? During Exploration, all those areas or centers you introduced can now be opened. If you are teaching alone at this time, you will want to supervise Exploration for Days 2 through 4. Your ultimate goal will be for students to work independently, with minimal supervision, so small groups can be pulled for targeted instruction. More on this later.

Each day, the areas or centers introduced during small-group instruction will be added to Exploration choices. Monitor students' progress at working independently. Redirect and retrain problem areas during Circle Time. Once Exploration runs smoothly, small-group instruction may be added.

During this time, decide what and to whom you wish to teach and in which subject(s). We might suggest Interactive Journals (see Chapter 5 on how to introduce and conduct this strategy). Or you can pull students who need certain skills for targeted instruction at their level. Refer to your literacy resource book for ideas.

Now that the basics are in place for Exploration time, you can introduce new activities to enrich the environment. Remember to first present and model each new addition during Circle Time. Examples of new activities:

- ◆ Simple art projects children can do on their own
- ◆ New toys or games
- ◆ A new story or tape at the Listening Center
- ◆ Big Book rereading center
- ◆ Read the room
- ◆ An observation center
- ◆ New puzzles
- ◆ A puppet center
- ◆ Alphabet stamps at the writing center

The list is endless!

End-of-the-Day Circle

Conclude Circle Time activities not yet completed. A top choice for day's end is—always—to read a story.

Dismissal

During the first two weeks, leave ample time for dismissal and walking to the bus loading zone. Allow time to spare. Always carry your class list!

FIRST TWO WEEKS OF SCHOOL—FIRST GRADE

Review the section on Kindergarten—First Day. Basically, you can follow this plan through the Opening Circle. For subsequent days, you might incorporate the following in Circle Times (review Chapter 5):

- ◆ Shared Writing: Morning Message
- ◆ Names Activities

During first grade, a significant time block is spent developing your student's literacy skills; therefore, the first two-week training period will appear somewhat different than kindergarten's. Your goal will be for students to work independently in Literacy Centers while you work with reading-based flexible groups. From the start, move your instruction toward having students become independent, self-directed learners—much easier said than done. Move slowly, stay with the training as long as necessary to instill independence and self-direction in your students. A sample schedule for first grade follows. Review your school's bell schedules for lunch and recess so you can determine how the time blocks will flow for you:

30 minutes:	Opening Circle
90 minutes:	Literacy Centers/Teacher-directed instruction to small flexible groups
30–45 minutes:	Circle: Names Activities or English Language Development
45–60 minutes:	Math Instruction/Math Centers
20 minutes:	Drop Everything and Read/Todo el Mundo a Leer
20 minutes:	Closing Circle

Day 1

Following Opening Circle, start the process for teaching students to work independently. Your ultimate goal will be to have small groups working independently at centers. However, start with the complete group. Plan whole-group activities until students demonstrate that they can manage a task independently and well.

Self-Portrait: Materials and Preparation

◆ Paper with enough space for a picture and three or four lines to write on: one per child

◆ Crayons

◆ Pencils

Procedure: Whole-Group Introduction

◆ Prepare a self-portrait on the same type of paper your students will use, but enlarge it on the copier to size 11 x 17. Show students the enlargement.

◆ Explain they will be drawing a picture of themselves and that you will demonstrate what is expected.

◆ Draw a picture of yourself. Talk about the details of your self-portrait as you draw.

◆ State that you will write something about yourself you want them to know about you. Think out loud about various things you might write:

"I think I'll write about my children. I have a son and a daughter. No, I think I'll write about my new haircut. It's really short, but it feels funny. Yes, that's it. I'll write, 'I have a new haircut. It's short. It feels funny because I used to have long hair.' "

◆ Model writing the message.

◆ Discuss expectations for how students will work on their own self-portraits. Involve them in a discussion of the appropriate way to work.

◆ Invite one volunteer to demonstrate how to obtain paper and walk to his or her seat. Have three or four students model; excuse the others to follow suit.

◆ Float among the class to monitor behavior; give specific praise for appropriate behavior. Your goal is to instill behavior. The self-portrait is secondary. Make your Freeze-and-Listen signal. Praise those complying with expected behavior.

◆ Instruct children to clean up before coming to the meeting area. Again, praise those following directions.

◆ Discuss how group time worked out. Inform students what you see they should work on. Role-play the solutions to your concerns.

You should stay with this whole-group structure for at least three days, but don't hesitate to remain in this mode for a week or more.

Other whole-group activities could be taken from the Kindergarten Small-Group Plan:

◆ Cubby names

◆ 3-D names

◆ Class book: At school, I like to _____ or _____. (Keep it simple.)

◆ Monthly writing sample to be posted on the wall

◆ Simple sequencing of pictures from a story you have read

◆ Copying or correcting Morning Message

◆ Page for any class book

The Next Step

Have the class work at two different activities. Divide classroom into two areas. Don't be concerned how desks and tables are grouped, only that there are two distinct areas. You will need to prepare two *different* activities: one to be done independently, and one involving you (for example, introducing the use of a tape recorder or computer). Do not become completely involved with this group, as you will also be needed to monitor the other group. Activities for the independent group should be based on the literature selection introduced at Circle Time. Some suggestions are sequencing pictures, drawing or writing reactions to the story, creating a classbook page based on a pattern. Keep the activity simple.

Introducing the Two Centers

- Divide the class in half randomly. Display a list showing the two student groups. Be sure students know *which* group they belong to and where to look if they forget.

- Devise a method for two distinct work areas in your classroom, each to accommodate one half of the class.

- Children need to see and hear what is expected at a given center. Oral explanations are not enough. Show where materials are stored, how they should be accessed, what to do at the center, where to put completed work, and so forth.

- Model the activities. These should include expected behaviors for your classroom community (e.g., where supplies are kept, how to obtain them, what product is expected, what to do when finished).

- Use a matching icon for each activity (e.g., use a pencil graphic for the writing activity, a book graphic for the sequencing activity).

- Dismiss one of the groups to Area 2. Praise children for walking quietly to the area and getting to work immediately. Or if they don't, bring them back and try again with one or two children modeling for the others. Then, try the whole group again.

- Send the other group to Area 1. You will want to work closely with this group on a more teacher-directed lesson but also be able to monitor Area 2.

- After twenty to thirty minutes, make the Freeze-and-Listen signal. Monitor cleanup behaviors. Praise specifically what students are doing correctly. Do not proceed until your standards are met.

- Before students move, remind them that they already know what to do in the new center—an important step in becoming independent. Instill that it is necessary to *listen* and know how to *follow directions*.

- Direct students to move to the other area.

- Repeat your lesson for Area 1; closely monitor Area 2.

- After twenty to thirty minutes, make the Freeze-and-Listen signal. Instruct students to clean up and proceed to the meeting area.

- Discuss results of work time. Inform students on what was well done and what requires more work. For at least one week, role-play behavior you want to see the next day. Each day, plan lessons requiring more of your involvement, then monitor if the other group works well independently. Do not try three groups until all students can work productively and independently without direct supervision.

See the *Teacher's Guide* of the literacy program adopted in your school for ideas, especially for independent groups. Refer to your literacy resource book for other ideas. Here are some additional ideas for a two-group rotation:

Area 1: Semi-Teacher-Directed	Area 2: Independent
Introduce equipment and materials, then allow time for practice	Make a page for a class book
Introduce Interactive Journals (see Chapter 5)	Reconstruct a poem or song. Illustrate it
Introduce Writing-Publishing Center	Practice handwriting
Read a story together. Do follow-up activity about the book	Work on name sorts (see Chapter 5)

Circle: Names Activities

During the first month of school, Names Activities in Chapter 5 should be included daily until each student has been delegated Student of the Day. Whole-group activity should take about twenty to twenty-five minutes. Remainder of the period should be spent with students writing their page for Student of the Day.

OR

Circle: English Language Development (ELD)

If there are English learners in your class, they should be provided with ELD at their levels of English language proficiency. Your principal can inform you of available curriculum materials. Read "Stages of Language Acquisition" (from *Into English! Teacher's Guide for Any Level*, by Tinajero and Schifini). Research whether any of your students have had language proficiency testing. List their names and levels. ELD instruction is very similar to the activities normally done at Circle Time, but instruction should be modified so all can understand and participate.

Drop Everything and Read (DEAR)/*Todo el Mundo a Leer (TEMAL)*

Children learn to read by reading. DEAR/TEMAL is a time when children should practice developing reading skills. As the year progresses, you can pull a small group for direct instruction during this time, provided it runs smoothly from the start.

Materials:

◆ Have a variety of books arranged for easy access. Book tubs work well in that all students do not have to go to the Library Corner to select a book.

Note: Students usually choose books with which they are familiar. Plan to place the books you have read aloud in the DEAR/TEMAL tubs.

◆ Have available books at your students' reading levels. They should have access to books read with you during Guided Reading. Arrange books of similar levels together.

- ◆ Include class-made books.
- ◆ Include student-authored books.
- ◆ Include magazines, catalogs, dictionaries, and the like.

Procedure:

- ◆ Have available at least twice the number of books available as there are students.
- ◆ Decide where and how they will read. Can they lie down? Must they stay in one area of the room? Can they read to one another?
- ◆ Conduct a class discussion on the treatment of books. A metaphor that works well is to liken a book to a baby. Ask if students would step on a baby, throw a baby, write on a baby, and so on. Emphasize that books should have the same treatment.
- ◆ Select one or two students to model how to choose a book carefully, then how a book should be read.
- ◆ Conduct a brief "book talk" about each of the books available. Briefly show the cover and read the title.
- ◆ Following that, have students close their eyes and visualize a book they would like to read. Ask for volunteers to share. Now, problem-solve methods for when two or more students wish to read the same book at the same time.
- ◆ Role-play solutions:
  - – Role-play what to do when you have finished one book and need another.
  - – Role-play how to put books away at the end of DEAR/TEMAL.
- ◆ Dismiss students individually to choose their books. Praise, praise, praise those who are reading.
- ◆ Monitor how this proceeds. Do not allow students to become restless or noisy. Make your Freeze-and-Listen signal the minute you sense students are not sustaining interest.
- ◆ Meet together as a group and discuss the results. Revisit problem areas; compliment successes.

During the first week, repeat this procedure daily. Briefly review the steps, but each day allow more responsibility so students can explain the activity to you. Praise, praise, and praise those who can articulate the process. By Week 2, if DEAR/TEMAL is running smoothly, start pulling students individually for assessments (see Chapter 2). If not, repeat the procedure until all are reading independently for a sustained period. Start assessments or small-group instruction only when this strategy is in place.

Note: Actual reading time should be increased each day until students can sustain their reading for thirty minutes without your intervention.

Math: 45–60 Minutes

Warm-up: Start each math lesson with a Warm-Up. This is done as a whole-class activity to quickly review known concepts. Here are some easy Warm-Ups for the first two weeks:

- Number 1–20 flashcards. Look and shout the number. Look and whisper the number.
- Number Flash: Prepare a transparency with dots for the numbers 1 through 6. Cut it apart. Flash a group of dots. Children shout out how many dots they see.
- Find squares: Draw a square on the chalkboard. Instruct children to look around the room and find squares. Share. Other days, they may find rectangles, circles, and triangles.
- Use any material and start a pattern (e.g., red, blue, and green). Invite children to help you make the pattern as long as necessary.
- Exercises: Decide on a movement (e.g., touch your toes). Show a numeral card. Children perform that number of matching movements. Change the exercise. Show another numeral.
- Teach a number fingerplay (see Chapter 6: Ten Elephants, Five Little Monkeys, etc.). Act it out.

Exploring Manipulatives

Most primary math programs begin with an introduction to all the math manipulatives students will encounter during the year. For the first two weeks, you will want to follow this:

- Prepare several tubs of the same manipulative (e.g., pattern blocks, linker cubes, Geoboards, Unifix cubes, etc.).
- Introduce that manipulative to the class. Discuss different things you can create with the manipulative. Model and have students model several ideas. Excuse students to work at tables.
- Monitor students at work. You may wish to make your Freeze-and-Listen signal and have students walk around the room to observe what others have created with their materials, then resume work.

Skill practice: Find in your adopted math program, or create, simple skill work sheets. Duplicate skill sheets for each student. Use these as the basis of a minilesson followed by individual student practice. Or use as assessment tools to determine what skills children bring into the classroom and what need to be taught.

Ideas for skill practice:
- Addition facts to 5
- Addition facts to 10

- ◆ Subtraction facts to 5
- ◆ Recognizing and writing numbers 1 through 100
- ◆ Completing simple repeating patterns

End-of-the-Day Circle

Remember to conclude Circle Time activities not already completed. Always consider reading a story as a top choice for ending the day. End of day should be calm, focused on what your students have learned and what they can anticipate the following day.

Dismissal

For the first two weeks, remember to allow plenty of time for dismissal and getting to the bus loading zone with time to spare. Always carry your class list!

FIRST TWO WEEKS OF SCHOOL— SECOND AND THIRD GRADES

Day 1

Getting Ready

Before students arrive at class, have your day's agenda visible for them in the same place you will display future agendas. If seating is assigned, place individual materials on each desk, whatever you feel is necessary for students' first days of school (pencils, crayons, math journals). On the board, you might write a simple letter with directions (e.g., "Dear Students, find your seat and introduce yourself to your neighbors.") Include your name. This sets a precedent for where students should look in the future for reminders, activities, and so on. The goal for Day 1 is to teach procedures and beginning routines. Reinforce that goal whenever you can.

Activities for the Day

All activities that will be referred to are described in detail in Chapter 5. Also, see Chapter 3 for sample procedural charts for each learning situation; detailed procedures for centers from the K–1 section may be useful. As students arrive and take their seats, make personal contact with each one. Introduce yourself to the students and also their parents, when present.

Attention Signal

After the bell rings for instruction to start, use your Freeze-and-Listen signal (see Chapter 3, "Routine and Procedures"). Start reinforcing the signal at once. Praise students who followed the directions and who stopped and looked at you. Review Freeze-and-Listen procedures; discuss each step on your chart.

Introductions: 10 Minutes

Introduce yourself to the students. Tell them something about yourself. Let them know you are as anxious as they are on the first day of school. Use this time to take attendance and lunch count, read any bulletins, and review the day's agenda.

Name Scramble 2: 45 Minutes

Explain the Name Scramble 2 activity (described in Chapter 5). For older students, you might include first and last names to unscramble, using upper-case letters so there are fewer clues. Have students sit on the floor as they finish unscrambling the name. Repeat procedures for sitting on the floor and for a teacher-led lesson. Display each student's name on tagboard strips and place in the center of the circle for all to read. Ask how students would attempt to alpha-betize the names. Follow their ideas until all names have been alphabetized. Reinforce your procedures! Now, sort names in other ways (e.g., number of letters, vowels, syllables, and the initial letter for boys or girls). Excuse students to return to their desks. Older students are usually more comfortable sitting at their desks. If so, use a pocket chart or masking tape for taping names to the chalkboard.

Letters: 20 Minutes

Explain: "Now that we know a little about each others' names, I want to learn more about what you like and dislike. I've written a letter to you about myself, and I want you to write a letter to me about you." Pass out your letter to the students, then read it aloud. Ask for a response in writing. Tell students where to turn in completed work (see Chapter 5 for complete directions regard-ing Letters activity). Keep letters as a baseline assessment for writing. (See Chapter 2, "Assessments," for using this information in your teaching.)

Getting Ready for Recess: 10 Minutes

Review how students should leave the classroom and also how they should come in when the bell rings. Where do they line up? Where do they have snacks? Review equipment and ball checkout procedures already in place. If time allows, try a sponge activity from Chapter 5, sing a song, or read a book.

Math Warm-Ups: 15–20 Minutes

After recess, before students enter the classroom, meet them in line or by the door. Praise positive behavior. When necessary, remind them of how to enter the classroom. Repeat procedures for working at their desks.

Math warm-ups are a transition activity used before each math lesson and are ten-minute practice sessions of computation operations students can do independently. Teach students the procedures, then explain and model the directions. Each student needs a math journal, whether teacher made or pur-chased. Create a transparency or large chart of a page from their math journals. Use either graph or regular lined paper, making sure your example matches the paper in the journals. Explain how students should date entries and write problems and how much of the page should be used. These organizational skills are not only useful for math warm-ups but can be used in other instructional areas. After reviewing the directions, write four to six computation problems most of your students can perform independently. Start with easy addition and subtraction facts, as their ability levels are not yet known to you. You are teaching the procedures now, not math skills. As students write and solve problems in their math journals, walk around, checking for their understanding of your directions. Using positive praise, reinforce procedures. Review answers to the problems on the board.

Math Activity: 30–40 Minutes

Graphing Activity: Before starting, review procedures for a teacher-led lesson. Ask the students what they know about graphs. Explain that they will create a graph using some of the sorting they have done, as with their names. All graphs represent data in a pictorial sense. Start with bar graphs. Write the title of the graph on the chalkboard, "Number of Letters in Our First Names." Draw a horizontal line near the bottom of the chalkboard. Beneath that line, write numbers 1 through 10, or several more than are in the longest name in the class.

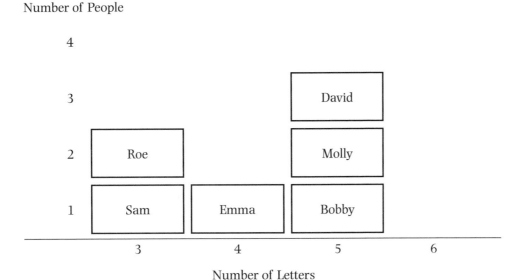

Number of Letters in Our First Names

Now, have students come to the board and tape their names (remember those tagboard strips?) in the appropriate spot on the graph. Reinforce the procedures. After all have participated, ask questions about the graph: How many students have four letters in their names? What is the least (or most) number of letters a student has in his or her name? Most have *how many* letters in their names? Ask them to explain something about the graph. Announce that they will continue with graphs the following day. If students have been sitting for some time, try a few stretches or a "moving" activity before proceeding. If time allows, they might decorate name tags, or that activity could be saved for after lunch.

Before Lunch: 10 Minutes

Review lunch procedures: Where do students eat? Are there special rules in the lunchroom? Review playground rules and procedures for returning to class. Use a name game from Chapter 5, sing a song, or do a sponge activity.

Read Aloud: 20 Minutes

Choose a book to read aloud. Explain read-aloud procedures as discussed in Chapter 3.

Social Studies: 30 Minutes

Do the Chapter 5 activity titled, "Know Your Classmates." Save worksheets for future Getting to Know You math graphing activities.

Jobs: 10–15 Minutes

Announce the classroom jobs you have assigned. Show and explain the system used to rotate jobs. Role-play how one does each job. Review cleanup procedures. While reinforcing procedures, allow students time for room cleanup.

PE: 25–30 Minutes

Explain procedures for outside behavior: where to meet, how to get there, signal for stopping, when to get drinks of water, and so on. Play a game from Chapter 5 or one you know. Explain procedures for returning to class. Reinforce procedures by using specific praise.

Closing: 15–20 Minutes

If homework is given on Day 1, take time to explain your system. Is homework returned the following day or at end of week? What are your expectations regarding neatness or help in editing from parents? This is a good time to send information home about your homework policy. Use the rest of the time to discuss their first day, sing a song, or try a sponge activity from Chapter 5.

Dismissal

At the door, say something pleasant to students as they leave. Use their names and smile. You made it!

Day 2

Scheduling

The first weeks include teaching classroom rules, procedures, and daily routines. *When* daily activities are scheduled is not as important as *consistency*. The lessons that follow are based on a schedule that includes transitions and builds toward encouraging independent learning.

Opening

Create a relaxed way to start the day—a place to take care of business and check in with students, blending into Morning Message. The key is to gauge class attentiveness. Keep it short. Combined Opening and Morning Message should take no longer than twenty minutes. After giving the Freeze-and-Listen signal, have students sit on the floor. Use positive praise to reinforce good behavior. Use this time to:

◆ Take roll and lunch count
◆ Ask a few students to share
◆ Review the daily schedule shown on the board
◆ Calendar (Chapter 3 has a more detailed account)
◆ Sing a song (see Chapter 6 for songs and fingerplays)
◆ Read a story or poem

If all these activities plus Morning Message take more than twenty minutes, then choose what works best for your class. Keep Opening to a minimum, as your voice will be taxed the first few days, explaining and reinforcing. Also, students find it hard to sit longer than twenty minutes.

Morning Message: 10 Minutes (see Chapter 5)

Use chart paper for your message. Work the text for capitalization, punctuation, and the use of margins. Discuss how the date is written. Keep it short. Write this message: "Good morning! Today we will learn more about each other. You will be doing paired interviews. Let's think of some good interview questions." Eventually, you can expand lesson time to include reading instruction by "working the text." Here are some starting points:

◆ New vocabulary, plurals, contractions
◆ Vowel patterns
◆ Deliberate mistakes in spelling or punctuation
◆ Spaces left blank to reinforce using contextual clues
◆ Omitted punctuation
◆ Margins, paragraphing

Literacy Activity: 30–40 Minutes

After working through the Morning Message text, discuss how an interview is conducted: Brainstorm good questions, reinforce procedures for a teacher-led lesson. Before starting interviews, gauge the time so students will not sit longer than twenty minutes. Pair students in advance; repeat behavioral expectations and procedures for this activity (see Chapter 5 for directions on Paired Interviews). After each partner has interviewed the other individually, form a group so every student may share what they learned about their partners.

Partner Draw: 45 Minutes

This is a cooperative art activity conducted with the same partners. Explain directions (see Chapter 5). Show where art materials are stored and model procedures for proper use. This activity will be the students' first art experience requiring procedures. Address these questions: Are students allowed to talk or leave their seats? Can they make negative comments about others' or their own work? What if they need to get supplies or to ask questions? What should students do when the activity has been completed? Artwork should not be shared until they have written about their drawings during writing time.

Before Recess: 10 Minutes

Clean up art supplies. Discuss and model procedures: Is this job shared or appointed? Give positive praise for correct behavior. Dismiss students for recess when the room is clean. Setting up the proper routines is the goal of this first week of school. Allow enough time to reinforce appropriate procedures. Have students sit on the floor while you read a story about cooperation or becoming acquainted with new people, if available. Discuss recess rules and equipment sign-out procedures. Reinforce where students should line up when the bell rings.

Writing: 30–40 Minutes

Continue to reinforce procedures for lining up or entering the classroom. Ask students to sit on the floor while you review teacher-led lesson procedures. Explain the writing process; discuss what they have previously learned about the process. Explain that they have already completed the prewriting step (drawing with partners) and will now begin the writing activity. Review procedures for working with partners. Ask partners to sit together and decide their format for writing about the drawing. After each pair has finished writing, have them share their story and artwork.

Math Warm-Ups: 10 Minutes

Write math warm-ups on the board; reinforce procedures.

Math: 45–60 Minutes

Continue the graphing unit. Remind students of yesterday's bar graph. Request ideas for recording data permanently. Quickly recreate the bar graph on butcher paper. Start using mathematical terms, such as bar graph, mode (most frequently occurring data), range (lowest to highest data), and mean (midrange). Ask the class, "What makes a good friend?" Following a short discussion, state that you will be collecting the data. Model how this is done. Create a chart of students' names. Ask each student the question; record his or her response by name. Start organizing data into a bar graph using labels and a title. Pair up students, have each pair copy the graph started on the board and complete it. Provide construction paper and markers. End math time by showing each graph.

Lunch

Clean up all materials and get ready for lunch. Review rules and procedures after the room has been organized.

Read Aloud: 15–20 Minutes

Reinforce procedures using praise. Read a book to the class.

Theme Activity: 45 Minutes

Introduce Me Pictures (see directions in Chapter 5).

Cleanup

Review procedures for room cleaning. Remind students of their jobs. You might role-play each job if there was not time for this yesterday.

PE: 30 Minutes

Review and reinforce procedures using positive praise. Play a class game.

Closing

Reflect on the day. Pass out and explain homework. Do a sponge activity.

Day 3

Opening and Morning Message

Literacy Activity

This morning block of time could, eventually, be used for reading centers. But until reading assessments have been completed, stay with whole-class lessons.

Names

The following activities focus on phonics and phonemic awareness, using the names of your students. Daily, select one to five names to work with, depending on your class's interest level and maturity. As students become acquainted with this routine, you might complete more than one or two names per day. When students start rolling around on the floor, *stop*, and have them stretch. The five names chosen will be your first words on the Word Wall.

Name Cheer: Ask each child to lead the class in a cheer for his or her name, saying, for example, "Give me an E, give me an M, give me an M, give me an A." Chant the letters in the name. Finish by shouting the child's name.

Letter Sort: Using students' names written on sentence strips, point to one of the letters in a name. Ask all students who have that letter at the beginning (end, middle, etc.) of their names to stand up. Decide if letters in the five chosen names have the usual sound for that letter.

Beginning Sounds: Use first and last names for this activity. Sort names according to the beginning letters up to the vowel. Point out how the same letter can have different sounds.

Clap the Syllables: Clap the syllables for each of the five names. Ask other students to stand up if their names have the same number of syllables.

Rhyming Words: Think of words that might rhyme with the student's name. Model rhymes for the class; have them join in.

Vowel Poster: Construct a poster showing all vowels, including "y." Sort names according to each vowel in that name. For example, "Emma" would be in both the "e" and "a" list. Discuss each vowel sound. Underline each vowel that has a sound; cross out all silent vowels.

Write the Names: Using half sheets of paper, ask students to write each person's name. Concentrate on proper letter formation.

Have the students create an acrostic poem by writing their names, one letter per line, going down the left side of the paper. Say, "Think of a word that describes you, beginning with that letter of your name." Or you might read a book about names, friendship, and so on.

Recess

Review procedures for leaving the classroom.

Writing: 30 Minutes

Start your journal routine (see Chapter 5). Explain journal writing. Brainstorm ideas for a journal. Explain journal time procedures. Consider individual brainstorming of interesting topics for the first entry. Have interested students share ideas or what they wrote. Ask them to recall yesterday's class graph on what makes a good friend. Request a story about a friend or a special time spent with a friend. Share. Collect journals to read and respond to. Reading and analyzing what students wrote can be used as mini-lessons for class or individual students.

Math Warm-Ups

Math: 45–60 Minutes

Refer back to the two class graphs; have students think of other questions that could be graphed. Brainstorm other graphing possibilities; record them on the board. Pair students up with new partners and have them choose either a class question or one they have decided on for collecting data and graphing. Partners collect data by asking classmates the question. Give each pair a class list to keep track of their work. Have construction paper and markers available for the pairs to create graphs. To complete the process, another math session will be needed. Review your graph criteria for title, labels, correct spelling, easy reading, and so on.

Lunch

Read Aloud

Social Studies: 45 Minutes

Do Shields activity described in Chapter 5.

Cleanup

Review procedures.

PE

Choose an activity from Chapter 5.

Closing and Homework Assignments

Day 4

Continue to reinforce routines and procedures. Use positive praise whenever possible.

Opening and Morning Message

Literacy Activity: 30–45 Minutes

Before starting, review and reinforce the Names activity, choosing one to five new names. Ask students to complete the Reading Self-Assessment (found in Chapter 2) followed by Find Someone Who, from Chapter 5.

Have students place journals on their desks before leaving for recess.

Writing: 30 Minutes

Continue the daily routine of Journals. Remind students of the procedures; request ideas for suggested topics. Gather students together to explain Wiggly Line (see Chapter 5 for complete directions).

Math Warm-Ups and Math: 45–60 Minutes

Continue graphing unit, allowing pairs more time to create their graphs.

Read Aloud

Social Studies: 45–60 Minutes

If necessary, allow students time to complete yesterday's shields. Have them pair up and share their shields. Display shields on a bulletin board. If time permits, play Bingo, shown in Chapter 5.

Cleanup, PE, Closing, Homework Assignments, Dismissal

Day 5

Opening and Morning Message

Sustained Silent Reading (SSR): 10–15 Minutes

Teach and model procedures for silent reading. Allow a few students at a time to choose books or place book tubs around the room to avoid crowding. Begin silent reading. Start with ten to fifteen minutes, increasing to twenty to thirty minutes by midyear. Reading progress is determined by how much and how long one reads. Use this time to individually assess reading skills and, later, for ongoing reading conferences or literature circles. (See Chapter 2 for "Assessments" and also for tips on teaching students how to choose books at the appropriate reading level.)

Literacy Activity: 30–45 Minutes

Continue with Names activities, choosing one to five different names. An activity such as fingerplay, basic stretches, or learning a song is needed at this point. Review procedures for your chosen activity beforehand. Gather students together on the floor. Read from a book showing a clearly stated beginning, middle, and end. (Before proceeding, review Instruction for English Language Learners in Chapter 2.) Together with your class, review each part of the book, including illustrations, listing their responses on chart paper. Discuss what is required for a good illustration and how one chooses a particular subject to represent the accompanying words. Also discuss how to choose the right caption for an illustration. Announce that tomorrow, they will complete a story sequence sheet.

Writing: 30 Minutes

Journals: Have students complete their self-assessment, *What I think About Writing*, found in Chapter 2. Have them store work in their portfolios to review for assessing.

Math Warm-Ups and Math: 45–60 Minutes

When graphs have been completed, share and display them. Pairs should choose a graph and write five sentences about the data. During the past few days, this project was modeled when questions were asked about class graphs. Examples: "More people have five letters in their names than have three letters;" "Dinner is the favorite meal of the people in our class;" "Volleyball has three fewer votes than baseball." Allow time for them to complete this task. Discuss each graph and what each pair has written.

Read Aloud

Social Studies: 30–45 Minutes

Introduce What Makes a Good Listener? Ask students why we should listen. Most will answer, "to follow directions or listen to the teacher." True, but here are more reasons to listen: pleasure and enjoyment (music, poetry, movies, nature, jokes, hearing a book read aloud), and also safety and communications (directions to a friend's house). Record their ideas. Ask for a student volunteer. Ask students to observe closely what you do and say. Whisper to the volunteer that as you model a poor listener, he or she should continue talking. Ask that child to tell you about his or her summer vacation for a few minutes. While your volunteer speaks, demonstrate poor listening by interrupting, asking irrelevant questions, playing with objects, not providing eye contact. Thank the volunteer. Ask if students noticed your actions, and ask how the volunteer might have felt. With another volunteer, demonstrate this exercise again by using good listening techniques. Thank that volunteer. Again, ask if students noticed your actions. Record responses; save the chart for future reference. Pair up students for good listening practices. Have partners take turns talking and listening. Suggest they talk about their summers or their dream vacations. Decide on a topic all might use. Have pairs decide who talks first. Allow two to three minutes for talking; signal when it is time to switch roles. Bring the class together to discuss their feelings and observations. Explain that a good characteristic of a *friend* is to be a *good listener*, an important skill for communicating with others.

Cleanup, PE, Closing, Homework Assignments

Dismissal

Today, send notes home requesting that each student bring a special object and a favorite book to school on specified days (Significant Object lesson is scheduled for Day 9; Favorite Book lesson for Day 10).

Day 6

Remember to Reinforce Procedures!

Opening, Morning Message, SSR

Literacy Activity: 45–60 Minutes

Continue Names activities by choosing one to five names to add to the Word Wall. Expand yesterday's lesson of story parts. Read aloud, choosing another book with a clearly defined beginning, middle, and end. Review each section orally. Have students return to their desks. Have them each fold a piece of paper into thirds, labeling the first section, "Beginning," the second section, "Middle", and the third section, "End." Then ask them to write about the parts of the book in the appropriate column. Ask them to share their work with the class; follow with a discussion of what goes into writing a good paper. Record their ideas for reference when this activity is repeated.

Journal

Writers' Workshop: 30–45 Minutes

Begin the workshop by reviewing the writing steps. Construct a chart showing key words or pictures (or both). Discuss how to decide on a topic and how this Writers' Workshop differs from Journal time. Students should have writing folders for their stories, individual dictionaries, and a list of commonly used words. Inform your teaching by assessing their stories. If many students are making the same errors, do a mini-lesson before each workshop period. If one student makes an error, correct that through an individual writing conference, after first making sure that your class has an understanding of all procedures.

Math Warm-Ups and Math: 45–60 Minutes

Using class graphs from the previous lesson, ask true-false questions about the graphs. Have students show thumbs up for true, thumbs down for false answers. Have pairs join again to write five or more true–false questions for their graphs, then share with the class using the thumb technique. Discuss how to determine a good question.

Read Aloud

Social Studies: "I" Messages: 45 Minutes (see directions in Chapter 5)

Pair younger students together rather than dividing them in groups of three or four. First, brainstorm problems that could occur or have occurred at school for pairs to use in their skits. Teach this format:

"I feel _____ (state the feeling), when you _____ (state the offending action), because _____ (state the consequence)."

Cleanup, PE, Closing, Homework Assignments, Dismissal

Day 7

Opening, Morning Message and SSR

Literacy Activity: 45 Minutes

Continue adding one to five names, followed by activities for each name. After about twenty days, all students' names will be included on the Word Wall. Start adding high-frequency words to the Word Wall. Follow this five-step format:

1. Each student should have paper or a word study notebook to write in the words.

2. As you say each word, students locate that word on the Word Wall. You then include each word in a sentence. After you have said the word, students should clap or snap each letter while spelling or looking at the word.

3. Ask students to write each word on paper or in their notebook. As they write the word, you write that word on the chalkboard or on the overhead projector screen.

4. Repeat for each word.

5. Each week, add five new words. Practice new words for a few days, making sure to review previously added words.

Start adding more difficult high-frequency words or homophones. Include other patterns, such as contractions, common blends, and vowel patterns, as well as *hard* and *soft* "c" and "g" words. Continue the Story Parts activity. Read another story to the class. Rather than discussing the beginning, middle, and end, have students return to their seats to complete the written assignment about the parts. Students then share their work, reinforcing criteria developed in class yesterday.

Journal, Writers' Workshop: 45 Minutes

Math Warm-Ups and Math: 45–60 Minutes

Use today and tomorrow for assessment. Choose a topic. Decide on the data, then have students create individual graphs for that data. Ideas: a favorite meal or season or the number of tickets sold by some students for the school carnival. When reviewing completed graphs, check for students' understanding of organization for that data. Are labels included? Is it titled? Is the work accurate? (See Chapter 2 for Informal Assessing.)

Read Aloud

Social Studies: Family Traditions: 45–60 Minutes

Discuss family traditions. Locate, then read aloud, *Family Pictures*, by Carmen Lomas Garza. Discuss the technique used for illustrating her book. Notice how entire pages are used for illustrations and the details in each drawing, including the clothing. If you cannot locate this book, describe one of your family traditions; use as many details as possible. Illustrate on the chalkboard how you might draw images of that tradition. Prepare a sample, either something you have drawn, an art print, or a magazine photograph. Have students illustrate traditions in their own families. Use an easily controlled art medium, such as markers, crayons, or colored pencils. Before starting, review the Art procedures.

Cleanup, PE, Closing, Homework Assignments, Dismissal

Day 8

Opening , Morning Message, SSR

Literacy Lesson: 45–60 Minutes

Continue working with words on the Word Wall. Add one to five names. If this task has been completed, review students' names. When moving into high-frequency words, review them before adding new words. Remaining time should be spent on the Family Traditions activity carried over from yesterday. Allow students time to complete their artwork, if necessary, but this day should be devoted to writing about the family tradition depicted in their drawings started yesterday. Tell or retell a story from your family. Have students describe or write about specific times their families were involved in the depicted traditions. Reinforce Writing Time procedures. Allow students time to share their art or stories (or both).

Journal and Writers' Workshop: 45 Minutes

Math Warm-Ups and Math: 45–60 Minutes

Use this time to continue assessing your students' understanding of graphing. Have them write five sentences about their graphs from yesterday. Follow that with asking them to write five true–false questions about their graphs. Collect and score papers; these will serve as good work samples for portfolios.

Read Aloud

Social Studies: 45–60 Minutes

Review "I" Messages. State examples of conflicts students might experience. Have each turn to a partner, then say the appropriate "I" Message for that situation. Explain that people communicate with language, by talking, or nonverbally, through use of body movements and voice tone. Demonstrate the following examples of nonverbal communication: arms crossed across your chest, hands on hips, finger shaking, a hug, smile, friendly pat on the back. Following each gesture, ask students what you are trying to communicate, then show how tone of voice can change a message from positive to negative. Try, "Oh, great!" with differing inflections to demonstrate excitement, or disappointment, or sarcasm. Have students reflect on the lesson: What did they learn? How would they sum it up? This can be done orally or by journal writing. Allow time for students to share.

Cleanup, PE, Closing, Homework Assignments

Remind students to bring a significant object for tomorrow's activity

Day 9

Opening, Morning Message, SSR

Literacy Lesson: Significant Object (see Chapter 5 for complete directions)

After an explanation of directions, allow pairs time to share, then have students write about their special or significant object. Have them share now or later in the day. Ask them to illustrate their objects. Bind stories together for a class book.

Journals and Writers' Workshop

Math Warm-Ups and Math

Start using math text.

Read Aloud

Social Studies

Continue yesterday's activity. Review "I" Messages, also verbal and non-verbal communication. Ask class to brainstorm emotions; write these on chart paper. If students cannot think of any, supply them yourself. Ask for antonyms for *happy* and *sad*. Before starting the lesson, have cards made up showing different emotions. Add to the stack any emotion words they might have thought of. Cards may be used in different ways:

- ◆ To alphabetize in pocket charts
- ◆ To illustrate each emotion and/or write about situations that could cause that emotion
- ◆ To act out, nonverbally, an emotion, for the class to guess.
- ◆ To form collages to depict that emotion, if you have access to magazines (ask students to choose an emotion, then cut or paste illustrations or photos from a magazine to illustrate it)

Cleanup, PE, Closing, Homework Assignments

Bring a favorite book for tomorrow's activity.

Day 10

Opening, Morning Message, SSR

Literacy Lesson: Word Wall

Continue to review high-frequency words added to the wall. Start the "Favorite Book" activity by sharing one of your favorites with the class. Read it aloud, then explain why you like the book. Ask for reasons why a person might like a particular book. Record responses on the board or chart paper. Have students write why the book they brought to school is a favorite. During SSR, make sure everyone brought a book. For those who did not, have them choose a class book to write about. Have them share their stories.

Journal and Writers' Workshop

Math Warm-Ups and Math

Read Aloud

Social Studies

Continue yesterday's activity. Choose an idea from Day 9.

Cleanup, PE, Closing, Homework Assignments, Dismissal

FIRST TWO WEEKS OF SCHOOL— FOURTH TO SIXTH GRADES

Day 1

All activities referred to in this section are described in detail in Chapter 5. (Also, see Chapter 3 for sample procedural charts for each learning situation.)

Getting Ready

Before students arrive, have the day's agenda written in the same place you will use it on a daily basis. If seating is assigned, you might place individual materials on each desk, whatever students should have during their first days at school (pencils, crayons, math journals, etc.). You might also write your name on the chalkboard and provide a simple letter with directions, such as "Dear Students, Please find your seat and introduce yourself to your neighbors." This sets a precedent for where students can find directions regarding future activities. Remember, today's goal is to teach *your* procedures and beginning routines. Reinforce that whenever possible.

As students arrive and take their seats, make personal contact with each one. Introduce yourself to students and also parents, if they are present.

Attention Signal: 5 Minutes

After the bell rings for instruction to begin, use your Freeze-and-Listen signal (see Chapter 3, "Routine and Procedures"). Start reinforcing the signal immediately. Praise those who followed the directions and stopped to look at you. Take a few minutes to repeat the Freeze-and-Listen signal and procedure. Discuss each step on the Freeze-and-Listen chart.

Introductions: 10 Minutes

Tell the students something about yourself. Explain that you are as anxious as they are on the first day of school. This is a good time to take attendance and lunch count, read any bulletins, and review the day's agenda.

Name Scramble 2: 45 Minutes

Explain the Name Scramble 2 activity, found in Chapter 5. Start by asking students to write five interview questions for the second part of this activity. Before passing out envelopes, model the interviewing process, making sure you have eliminated those for students who are not present. Envelopes might include first or last names to unscramble. Use all upper-case letters so there are fewer clues. Allow four to five minutes to unscramble names and transition students to the interviews. Give a two-minute warning before moving to introductions. Have students make introductions in alphabetical order by *first* name. Before starting, brainstorm a good strategy with them. If a pocket chart is available, students can come forward and place letters in the chart. Use masking tape for taping names to the chalkboard, or students could simply write names on the board as they come up for introductions. Follow the procedures for closure.

Letters: 20 Minutes

Explain:

"Now that we know something about each others' names, I want to learn who *you* are. I've written you a letter about myself, and I'd like you to write me about yourselves. You can include hobbies, family information, what subjects you particularly like in school, and what you're looking forward to this year."

After passing out your letter, read it aloud. Have them write you their letters, using your letter as a model format. Record a skeleton letter format on the board for students to follow. Explain where their completed work should be turned in and what to do while others are completing their letters. (See Chapter 5 for complete directions on Letters activity. This is a great baseline assessment for writing. Chapter 2 also shows how this information can be used in teaching). Begin a portfolio for each student. Attach the rubric score to their letters (see Chapter 2, "Writing Expectations") and also, a monthly writing sample. Place these in each folder and you'll be ready for report cards, with work samples for parent conferences.

Getting Ready for Recess: 10 Minutes

Review how students should leave the classroom and how they should enter when the bell rings. Where do they line up? Where do they have snacks? Review any equipment or ball checkout procedures in place. If time allows, do a sponge activity from Chapter 5, or read from a book.

Math Warm-Ups: 15–20 Minutes

Before students come into class, meet them in line or at the door. Praise positive behavior—or remind them of the proper way to enter the room. Review procedures for working at desks.

Math warm-ups are a transition activity before each lesson—a ten-minute computation practice of operations and problem solving that students can do independently. Teach them the procedures, then explain and model the directions. Each student needs a math journal (purchased or created by the teacher). Using a page like that in their math journals, make an overhead projection image or large chart. Use either graph or regular lined paper, but the example must be on the same type of paper as the students will use. Demonstrate how to date entries and write problems and how much space should be used. These organizational skills are not only important for math warm-ups but also for other instructional areas. After reviewing directions, write four to six computation problems most of the students can perform independently. Start with easy regrouping and multiplication problems, as their ability levels are still unknown. Also, you are teaching *procedures and directions*, not *math skills* at this point. As students write and solve problems in their math journals, walk around, checking for their understanding of your directions. Review answers to the problems on the board.

Math: 40 Minutes—Graphing Activity

First, review procedures for a teacher-led lesson. Explain that students will start a unit on graphs. Ask what they know about graphs. Record in the "Know" column on a chart similar to this one:

Graphs

Know	Want to Know	Learned

Then, ask what they would like to know about graphing, and record their answers. Explain that you will record what they have learned at the end of the unit and that graphing is used to organize data, record information, and generate answers to questions. There are several types of graphs, all representing data in a pictorial sense. If possible, show examples of bar, line, circle, and picture graphs. (Consider this homework assignment: Have students cut graphs from the newspaper, then create a display showing questions about each graph.) Explain that they will start by designing a bar graph that uses their names. Post a graph similar to the following one in an easily accessed place:

How Long Are Our Names?

1	2	3	4	5	6	7	8	9	10

Ask each student to write the number of letters in their first name on 3 x 3 Post-it notes or on 3 x 3 tagboard pieces. Reinforce the procedures. Ask that students who have one letter in their name come forward, then two letters, and so on, until the bar graph has been completed. After all have participated, ask questions about the graph: *What's the least or most number of letters in a student's name? Which number occurs most often?* (This is called the mode). Start a vocabulary chart of graph terms; post the chart. Ask that students write four summary statements about the graph in their math journals; have students share some of these. Announce that graph work will resume tomorrow. If time allows, students can decorate name tags—or save that activity for after lunch.

Please/Please Don't: 30 Minutes

This activity supports the development of classroom rules. (See Chapter 5 for instructions.)

Before Lunch: 10 Minutes

Review lunch procedures: Where do students eat? Any special lunchroom rules? Review playground rules and procedures for returning to class. If there is time, students could decorate name tags or do a sponge activity from Chapter 5.

Lunch

Read Aloud: 20 Minutes

Choose a book from the list in Chapter 8 or one of your own. Explain read-aloud procedures, as discussed in Chapter 3.

Social Studies: 30 Minutes

Do the activity from Chapter 5: Know Your Classmates.

Homework: 10 Minutes

Explain your homework system. Is homework returned the next day or at week's end? What do you expect in terms of neatness, editing, parental help, and so on? This is a good time to send information home about your class, including your homework policy. Explain today's homework assignment. During the first week or first month of school, provide each student with a blank calendar. Assign homework for that day and have students write the assignment in the appropriate box. Walk around and monitor. Demonstrate with an overhead projection of the calendar. Suggested homework for the first night: Have parents sign all school forms; bring in a book for SSR.

Cleanup: 10–15 Minutes

Discuss the assigned classroom jobs. Demonstrate and explain the system used for rotating jobs. Role-play how to perform each job. Review cleanup procedures. Allow time for cleanup while you reinforce the procedures. (See Chapter 3 for additional cleanup procedures.)

PE: 20–30 Minutes

Explain procedures for outside activities: where to meet, how to get there, the signal for stopping, when to get drinks of water, and so on. Play a game described in Chapter 5 or one that you know. Explain procedures for returning to class. Reinforce those who are following procedures by using specific praise.

Closing: 10 Minutes

Reflect on the day. Ask students to respond to the following prompts, first with a partner, then by sharing with the class:

◆ Name three things you learned today.

◆ Name two things you look forward to tomorrow.

◆ Name one thing you might share with a friend or your family.

Dismissal

Standing at the door, say individual good-byes to students as they leave. Use their names and smile—you made it!

Day 2

Scheduling

The first weeks of school are about teaching your classroom's rules and procedures, also your daily routines. *When* daily activities are scheduled is not as important as being *consistent*. Lessons shown in the following schema are based on a schedule that includes transitions and encourages independent learners.

Opening: 10 Minutes

This is a relaxed way to start the day—a place to do business and check in with your students—and blends into Sentence Corrections or Journals (see directions in Chapter 5). The key is to gauge your class's attentiveness—and keep it short. Combined Opening and the Transition activity should take not longer than twenty minutes.

Give the Freeze-and-Listen signal. Appreciate the class for getting quiet quickly. Review Opening procedures shown on the chart in Chapter 3. Take roll and lunch count and review the day's schedule, shown on the board.

Sentence Corrections: 30 Minutes

(See directions in Chapter 5.) This activity starts with a mini-lesson in writing. Analyze student errors from Day 1's writing activity. For the mini-lesson, choose one or two punctuation, capitalization, or spelling errors to focus on. Write a sentence on the board that has several errors. Work the text with students, inviting them to think aloud about correcting the errors. Here are some starting points:

◆ New vocabulary, plurals, contractions

◆ Capitalization

◆ Deliberate mistakes in spelling or punctuation

◆ Omitted punctuation

◆ Margins, paragraphing

Students will each need a journal for daily writing activities. Explain your procedures for Sentence Corrections; continue with the activity as described in Chapter 5. You might close by asking students to write the response to a prompt: for example, "What I know about plurals;" "How I'll remember the spelling of 'their,' 'there,' and 'they're;' " or "I know when to begin a new paragraph when _____."

Literacy: 45 Minutes

Introduction: Read "My Name," p. 10, from *House on Mango Street*, by Sandra Cisneros. Ask students for personal responses to the story. (Note: if copies or specific chapters are available, this can become your first literature study and also serve as a springboard to a writing project).

Instruction: Brainstorm the types of information Sandra Cisneros gave us about her name. Explain that students are to write about their names and then share within a small group.

Guided practice: Allow students time to write the "story of their names." Have them share, one at a time, in small groups.

Closure: Ask students to share something interesting they learned about their classmates.

Preparation for Recess

No one leaves until the classroom has been cleaned up! Students should follow both routine and procedures. Discuss recess rules and equipment sign-out procedures. Remind where they are to line up when the bell rings.

Recess

Math Warm-Ups: 15 Minutes

Continue reinforcing these procedures.

Math: 45 Minutes

Continue the graphing unit. Remind students of yesterday's bar graph. Start using mathematical terms: *bar graph*, *mode* (most frequently occurring data), *range* (lowest to highest data), and *mean* (midrange). Write these words on a vocabulary chart; add to the chart throughout the unit. Brainstorm with students strategies to help them remember each word's meaning. Explain that there are three major types of graphs. These can be designed from *opinions*, *facts*, or data requiring *processing* before being recorded. Share one to two examples of each; brainstorm others until you have at least six or seven examples in each category. When students design their own graphs, they will choose from this list of questions. Some examples follow.

Opinions:

- Did you like the new Star Wars movie?
- What career would you like?

Facts:

◆ In what month were you born?

◆ How many people are there in your family?

Process:

◆ How high is your plant today?

◆ If a = 1, b = 2, c = 3, and so on, how much is your first name worth?

◆ How much rainfall have we had each day this week?

Ask students, "What kind of graph is How Long Are Our Names?" Inform them, "Today, we will make another bar graph, and again, data will be recorded horizontally." Choose an opinion question for today's data collection. Model how data should be collected; work from a class list of student names. Ask each student the question; record the response by his or her name. Using labels and a title, start organizing data into a bar graph. Pair the students; have each pair copy the graph started on the board, then complete it. Provide rulers, markers, and white construction paper. (You might have to demonstrate use of a ruler.) When graphs are completed, fill in the chart you started. Ask students for mode, range, and mean, then record them. Have them write five summary statements about the graph, neatly, at bottom of the data. (See the following example.)

What Career Interests You?

Health	Karen	Rich			
Computers	Juan				
Sports					
Business					
Education					

Summary

1. _____

2. _____

3. _____

4. _____

5. _____

Please/Please Don't: 30 Minutes

(For Day 2 of this activity, see directions in Chapter 5). The purpose of this activity is to introduce students to your class rules, which are based on how students wish to be treated. During this time, explain your consequence system. Include both positive and negative consequences. (See Chapter 3 for ideas.)

Examples of positive consequences:

◆ Group points for being at task and being ready

◆ Group with the most points is dismissed first for activities, and so on

Example of negative consequences, in ascending order of seriousness:

1. Warning
2. Time out (with work) in class
3. Time out (with work) in another classroom or during recess
4. Call home
5. Meet with parents, develop behavior contract

Lunch Preparation

Reinforce procedures, get ready for lunch.

Lunch

Read Aloud

Social Studies: 30 Minutes

Introduce Partner Drawings. (See Chapter 5 for directions.) Also, you should explain where art materials are kept and procedures for using them. This is their first art experience in your class. Review procedures: Can students get out of their seats? Are they allowed to talk, say negative comments about others' or their own work? What if they have a question or need supplies? What should they do when the project has been completed?

Cleanup

Clean up the art supplies. Go over procedures needed for this: Do certain people have this job, or does everyone help? Remember to reinforce procedures and give positive praise.

Homework

Pass out and explain the homework. Students should record it on homework calendar.

Cleanup

Review cleanup procedures. Remind students of their jobs. Role-play each job, if time did not allow for it yesterday.

PE

Review procedures. Play a class game.

Closing and Dismissal

Reflect on the day. Do a sponge activity.

Day 3

Opening

Journals: 15 Minutes

Begin journal routine (see Chapter 5). Discuss: What is journal writing? Brainstorm what might be written in a journal. Review journal time procedures. The first entry might be individual brainstorming of interesting topics. Have interested students share their ideas or what they wrote. Ask students to recall yesterday's class graph, "What makes a good friend." Invite them to write about a friend or special time with a friend. Have them share. Respond to several journals during writing time, or respond after collecting the journals. Reading and analyzing what students write is a good source both for mini-class lessons and individual instruction.

Literacy

Read "The House on Mango Street," p. 3, from *The House on Mango Street.* Deconstruct the story by filling in a mind map on the board similar to this example:

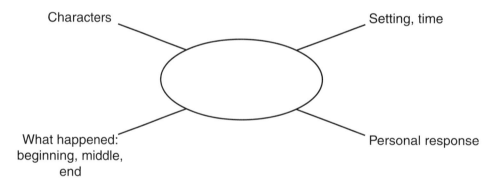

Tell students they will begin their own Memorable Moment story, starting with a mind map, then outlining the event. Those who finish early can add illustrations to their mind map.

Recess

Math Warm-Ups: 15–20 Minutes

Math: 45–60 Minutes

Refer back to the two class graphs. Inform students they will work in pairs and follow these steps for designing a bar graph:

◆ Decide on a question from yesterday's list.

◆ Predict some outcomes. Record the predictions (show students where to record them).

◆ Gather data on a class list.

◆ Organize information for placing on graph.

◆ Display information on graph; include title and labels.

◆ Interpret the graph with three summary statements.

◆ Write the mean, range, and mode beneath summary statements.

Model the Process

Pair the students; have them choose one class question. Have pairs collect data by asking their classmates the question. Give each pair a class list to keep track of responses. Have construction paper, rulers, and markers available for pairs to use in creating graphs. Review criteria for a good graph: a title, easy-to-read labels, correct spelling, three statements about the graph, and the mean, range, and mode.

Name Games, Initial Adjectives: 20 Minutes

See directions in Chapter 5.

Lunch

Read Aloud

Social Studies

Do Shields activity described in Chapter 5.

Homework, Cleanup, PE, Closing, Dismissal

Continue to reinforce routines and procedures. Use positive praise whenever possible.

Day 4

Opening

Sentence Corrections

Literacy

Continue with the writing project, Memorable Moment. Today's reading is "Laughter," p. 17, from *The House on Mango Street*, by Sandra Cisneros. Begin by introducing it as a story about an experience with a sibling. Ask students to think about such an experience, then share with a partner. Students should have a copy of the story and can read with partners or silently. After they have read it, ask what they clearly visualized or pictured in their minds from this story. Have students read aloud any particularly descriptive phrases or passages. Discuss descriptive writing. As students develop their stories, have them focus on making pictures with their words. Pair students. Have them orally relate their stories (based on mind maps) to each other. Model this process with your story. Have students write their first draft. Announce they will get feedback and editing help from their partners before writing their final copy.

Preparation for Recess

Before students leave, have them place their SSR books on their desks. Tell them they will read silently for twenty minutes when they return.

Recess

SSR: 20 Minutes

Start to teach procedures for the daily routine of silent reading (see Chapter 3 for SSR procedures). Students might record their reading and responses on a Reading Log (see example). There is a direct relationship between reading progress, how much one reads, and performance on standardized tests. One hour per day is ideal. When students can follow procedures, start Oral Reading and Comprehension Assessments, described in Chapter 2. Include results of individual assessments in student portfolios. Note tips on how students can choose a book at their reading level.

Reading Log

Date	Title and Author	Comments	Pages Read

Math Warm-Ups and Math

Introduce a Line Graph, explaining that this graph is used to chart information over time. Line graphs require some processing before recording data. Show the following example replicated on a large piece of chart paper:

Dave's TV Watching

	Monday	Tuesday	Wednesday	Thursday	Friday
5 hours					
4 hours					
3 hours					
2 hours					
1 hour					

Ask students for summary statements about this graph; record them in math journals. Turn statements into questions (as preparation for the final project). Ask students to write some conclusions in their journals based on their interpretation of the data. Explain that it is important to justify their thinking when using the numerical information they have analyzed. Share some responses. Generate a list of things they do daily that might be charted over the next week. Have students decide on what they will individually chart. Provide recording sheets; explain that for homework next Tuesday, they will be developing line graphs with their data.

Partner Surveys: 40 Minutes

Do Partner Surveys, found in Chapter 5. This activity provides valuable information about your students' backgrounds, interests, and experiences that can be used to inform future curriculum planning.

Lunch

Read Aloud

Social Studies

Give students time to complete their shields from yesterday, if necessary. Have them pair up to share their shields. Display shields on a bulletin board. If time allows, play Bingo, from Chapter 5.

Homework Assignment, Cleanup, PE, Closing, Dismissal

Day 5

Opening

Journals

See the Journal prompt idea in Literacy.

Literacy

Today's lesson focuses on "*A Rice Sandwich,*" p. 43, from *The House on Mango Street*. Start by asking students to recall a time when they convinced their parents to let them have something they really wanted. They might use this as a quick write in their journals for an introduction to the lesson. Have some students share stories with the class, or have them share with partners. Read the story aloud, in pairs, at table groups, or individually. Follow the reading by asking students if any words need clarification. Use context clues in the sentence to define them. Pose discussion questions such as, "Why did Esperanza want to eat in the canteen?" "How did she convince her mom?" "Why did Sister Superior allow her to stay that day?" "How did Esperanza feel about the experience?" To encourage full participation, have students discuss their responses in small groups. Ask one person to summarize the story, then ask for predictions of what could happen next (as in a sequel if the story were continued). Post these words on a chart for reference: *clarifying, questioning, summarizing,* and *predicting.* Students then continue and complete first drafts of their Memorable Moment story. Be sure you have activities and procedures for those who finish early.

Recess

SSR

Math Warm-Ups and Math

Check in with students regarding their line graphs. Ask what each is going to chart; get a sampling of how they are doing thus far. Introduce a circle graph. Show a sample; brainstorm the distinguishing features of a circle graph. Record the ideas on a chart.

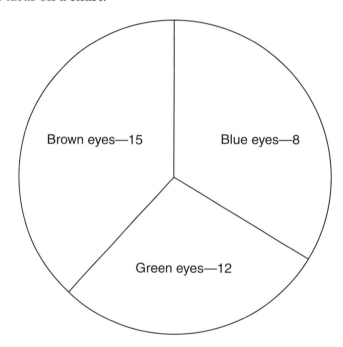

Summarize what the circle graph shows. Discuss *when* one might display data on a circle graph and *why* this graph would be used in place of a line or bar graph. Working with students, create a circle graph that follows these procedures:

- ◆ Decide on a question from the class list.
- ◆ Predict what the outcomes might be. Record the predictions.
- ◆ Gather data on a class list. (Start the process; have students finish it in pairs).
- ◆ Organize information to place on a graph.
- ◆ Display information on the graph; include title and labels.

- Have each student copy the graph, then write five questions about the graph.
- Students exchange graphs and answer each other's questions.

Provide students with a class list, construction paper, rulers, and markers for creating graphs. Close by discussing questions and answers.

Survey: What I Think About Math: 15 minutes

This survey will provide important information about students' attitudes toward math. (See Chapter 2 for the survey.)

Lunch

Read Aloud

Social Studies: What Makes a Good Listener?

Ask students why we should listen. Most will answer, "to follow directions or listen to the teacher." True, but here are more reasons to listen: pleasure and enjoyment (music, poetry, movies, nature, jokes, hearing a book read aloud), and also safety and communication (directions to a friend's house). Record their ideas. Ask for a student volunteer. Ask students to observe closely what you do and say. Whisper to the volunteer that as you model a poor listener, he or she should continue talking. Ask that child to tell you about his or her summer vacation, or something similar, for a few minutes. While your volunteer speaks, demonstrate poor listening by interrupting, asking irrelevant questions, playing with objects, not providing eye contact. Thank the volunteer. Ask if students noticed your actions, and ask how the volunteer might have felt. With another volunteer, demonstrate this exercise again by using good listening techniques. Thank that volunteer. Again, ask if students noticed your actions. Record responses; save the chart for future reference. Pair up students to practice good listening. Have partners take turns talking and listening. Suggest they talk about their summers or a dream vacation. Decide on a topic all might use. Have pairs decide who talks first. Allow two to three minutes for talking; signal when it is time to switch roles. Bring the class together to discuss their feelings and observations. Explain that a good characteristic of a friend is to be a good listener, an important skill for communicating with others.

Homework

Send notes home requesting that students bring in three special objects for the Graffiti Board lesson the following Wednesday.

Cleanup, PE, Closing, Dismissal

Day 6

Opening

Sentence Corrections: 30–40 minutes

For today's lesson, focus on the story, "And Some More," p. 35, from *The House on Mango Street*. Start by asking what students know about using dialogue in writing. Record their answers. Give each student a copy of the story. Ask them to read it silently or with partners, or you may read it aloud. Ask what they noticed about the author's use of dialogue and why the author might *not have used* quotation marks. Using the text as an example, demonstrate where *you would use* quotation marks for dialogue. Students then use the text to fill in quotation marks. Correct at least one page together.

Literacy: 45 minutes

Model the process of providing feedback on first drafts. Explain that students will work in pairs—one reads his or her story to the partner. The Listener will listen quietly until the Author has finished. Listener then tells two positive things about the story and asks one question for clarification. Model the process with your story. Brainstorm with the class about stems that indicate positives, as well as about question stems. Record these on a chart for reference, adding to them over time.

Examples:

- ◆ I really liked the part _____.
- ◆ Your description of the _____ was _____.
- ◆ I wondered how old you were when _____.
- ◆ What did you mean when you said _____ ?

Partner the students, allowing fifteen minutes for feedback. Monitor partners; remind them to switch after seven minutes. Have students record the feedback at the bottom of their drafts so it can be used for revisions. Close by requesting comments, insights, and questions.

Recess

SSR

Start Oral Reading and Reading Comprehension Assessments, as described in Chapter 2, if not already begun. You might accomplish two assessments during a twenty-minute SSR period. Students must follow SSR procedures to allow you to work with individuals.

Math Warm-Ups and Math

Start the graphing project. They will work individually on this project; explain that graphs are due on Day 9. Give students the following guidelines in writing.

- Decide on a topic for your graph. Think of a question to match your topic.
- Using the class list to record data, survey each class member.
- Decide which type of graph would best display your information: bar, line, or circle.
- Using pencil, make a rough draft of your results. Have a friend check your graph. Be sure it meets the criteria of a good graph.
- Using a ruler and thin markers, make a final copy, including title, your name, due date, labels, and pictures relating to your topic.
- Below the graph, write five questions relating to your graph.
- On the back of your graph, write answers to the questions.
- Attach a paragraph describing some conclusions you have drawn from your graph results. Use numeric data to justify your opinions.

Allow students time to decide on topics and questions and to start surveying classmates.

Survey: What I Think About Reading

There may be time before lunch to conduct an attitude survey on reading. Refer to Chapter 2 for the actual survey.

Lunch

Read Aloud

Social Studies

For complete instructions, see "Conflict Resolution: 'I' Messages" in Chapter 5. Explain to students that you will teach them a way to work out problems with others. This method can be used in all situations for the rest of their lives. Share frameworks for problem-solving language:

- I didn't like it when _____ because it made me feel _____.
- I'm sorry that I (or I'm sorry that you feel) _____. Next time, _____.

A situation becomes diffused when the person with the problem feels *heard* by another. Explain that a respondent may not answer a problem with another one—she or he may not respond in this manner: "Well, I didn't like it when *you* _____, either!"

Problem solvers may only work on one problem at a time. Put sentence frames on the board or a poster. Continue with Problem-Solving Skits as described in Chapter 5. Laminate both the problem-solving process and language frames on 4 x 6 cards. Place them in an envelope near the door. Explain that when students have something to work out with another, they first check with the teacher, then each takes a card before stepping outside to quietly resolve their situation. Allow a maximum time frame of five minutes; use only for one-on-one situations.

Problem-Solving Process	Problem-Solving Language
Person introducing the problem:	
1. Identify the problem:	"I don't like it when _____."
2. Tell how it makes you feel:	". . . because it makes me feel _____."
3. If appropriate, tell why it bothers you:	"It bothers me because _____."
Person responding:	
1. Take a moment to think about it.	Silence; thinking time
2. Use diffusing words:	"I'm sorry that I _____." "I'm sorry you feel _____."
3. Tell what you will try to do next time:	"Next time, I'll try _____."

Homework, Cleanup, PE, Closing, Dismissal

Day 7

Opening, Journals

See Literacy activity for possible journal prompt.

Literacy

For this lesson, use the story, "The First Job," p. 53, in *The House on Mango Street*. Start by asking students to describe their first job. They might do a quick write about this experience during journal time, sharing with a partner or with the whole class. Have them read the story in groups of four: Students number off, one to four. Ask groups to reach consensus on how they wish to read the story: one person reading the whole thing aloud, taking turns reading aloud paragraph by paragraph, or everyone reading silently.

Follow the reading by asking if anyone needs to clarify a word. Write words on the board. Ask groups to choose three words from the list to clarify, using context clues in the sentence. In each group, the student who is Number 1 leads the word-defining process.

Next, ask the class to generate questions about the story. Record these on the board. Model the process of being a student facilitator: Choose a question for discussion and ask students to take turns responding to the question in their small groups, with Number 2s acting as the facilitators. If a group finishes before time is called, it can start on another question. Next, have the groups summarize the story, with student Number 3 leading this part of the exercise. Last, each group member is to predict a sequel to the story, with student Number 4 leading this section. Between each process, have groups share several responses with the whole class. For closure, ask groups to self-assess how they worked as a group. A survey form could be developed, with questions and a rating scale showing member participation, performance of roles, future improvements, problems to be solved by the group, and so on.

Recess

SSR

Writer's Workshop

Reading activities will soon fill the morning block; writing can be moved to the time period following SSR. Ask students, working in pairs, to peer-edit each other's first drafts before moving to final drafts. Create a peer-editing form that reminds the editor to search out the title, underline spelling errors, mark punctuation and capitalization errors, and check for correct paragraphing. Allow space for the editor to sign his or her name. Teach editing marks to be used on a consistent basis and post these on a chart. Give students individual copies to staple in their writing journals. Have students turn in rough drafts to you for editing before writing final copies.

Math Warm-Ups and Math

Begin by developing a rubric of criteria to be used for self-assessment of their graphs and your assessment of students' work. Ask them to refer to guidelines defined yesterday.

Put up a large chart to record student ideas. Ask students to describe components of a graph that would meet all guidelines. Record them in Column 3 (see example to follow).

1	2	3
		Title neatly written with thin marker. Five questions on the bottom, clearly numbered. Five answers written on the back, clearly numbered. And so on

Have students describe a graph that would be assessed as a "1." Record descriptions in Column 1. Then, ask what a "2" would look like; record answers in Column 2. Allow students time to work on their graphs.

Lunch

Read Aloud

Social Studies

Do the Appreciation Words activity, described in Chapter 5. Follow with Graffiti Boards, using the three objects each student brought in on Monday.

Homework, Cleanup, PE, Closing, Dismissal

Day 8

Opening and Sentence Corrections

Literacy

Begin with a portion of core literature or a short story, using the reading process described in Day 7. Introduce the story through theme, predictions, book jacket, and so on. Have students read to a certain point, deciding together how that section should be read. Invite class to generate words to be clarified; record them on the board. Ask Number 2 students to lead their group in defining words. Model, then check for understanding. Share definitions. Ask groups to generate questions about the selection and share them with the whole group; record them. Number 3 students are to then choose a question and facilitate the discussion in their groups. Share several discussion highlights with the whole class. Number 4 students then lead the summarization; Number 1 students lead predictions for the next section. Close by asking for personal connections with the story's theme thus far.

Recess

SSR

Writer's Workshop

Return students' papers with your edits; have them write final drafts. Provide appropriate paper, decide whether students should use pencil or pen, whether to print or write in cursive, and where illustrations should be placed. Announce that they will illustrate their stories tomorrow.

Math Warm-Ups and Math Lesson

Have students complete graph projects. Have something ready for those who finish early.

Lunch

Social Studies

Continue Problem-Solving Skits from Chapter 5, begun on Day 6. Give instructions, then explain that people communicate 75 percent of what is said by nonverbal actions, with our bodies or tones of voice. Demonstrate examples of nonverbal communication by using your body: a hug, smile, friendly pat on the back, arms crossed against the chest, hands on hips, the shake of a finger, and so on. Following each gesture, ask students what you are trying to communicate. Now, show how tone of voice can change a message from positive to negative. Try, "Oh, great!" with differing inflections that can mean excitement, or disappointment, or sarcasm. Invite students to integrate nonverbal language into their skits. Following skits, have students reflect on what was learned— either orally or by journal writing. Have them share.

Homework, Cleanup, PE, Closing, Dismissal

Day 9

Opening and Journals

Literacy

Continue reading the piece of literature begun yesterday, or introduce a new short story. You might start by summarizing where yesterday's story left off, with predictions for today. If working with a new piece of text, introduce the story's theme, connecting it with students' lives. Rotate roles: Today's Number 3s will lead the defining of words, Number 4s will be the facilitators, Number 1s will lead the summarizing, and Number 2s will ask for predictions. Explain that, after following today's reading (a modified version of Reciprocal Teaching), each person in each group will be responsible for recording something. Lead the class through the four steps: clarification of vocabulary words, discussion, summarizing, and predicting. Provide work sheets for each role; give work sheets to the appropriate students. Allow time for the Clarifiers to record sentences, with chosen words underlined and definitions generated by the group. Discussion directors are to record the discussion question and the group's responses. Summarizers record the group's summary; Predictors record the group's predictions. Allow time for sharing with the whole group; reflect on the activity and also the group process. Model the four recording tasks on an overhead projector screen. Before proceeding, check to see that all the students understand what they are supposed to do.

Recess

SSR

Writer's Workshop

Students illustrate their stories. Provide a variety of art materials. Make sure students know your procedures for acquiring and using materials and cleaning up. Before they start drawing, you might use picture books to model a variety of illustrative styles.

Math Warm-Ups and Math Lesson

Return to the original KWL chart. Ask students to write what they have learned in this graphing unit. Encourage sharing and record comments on the class chart. Give students a typed copy of the rubric they developed yesterday. Have them self-assess their graph by following the rubric's criteria, underlining those elements that reflect their work. Below the rubric, leave space for students to write the score they feel they deserve and why. Leave another space for students to write a personal goal for their next math project. Have them trade their graphs with a partner. Each student should read the partner's graph and answer the five questions (without looking on the back!). Students return graphs to their owners, who then correct the paper. Allow time for pairs to discuss their work. Explain that you will score graphs on a separate rubric, attaching it to theirs. Post the graphs, and you are ready for Back to School Night!

Lunch

Read Aloud

Social Studies

Continue yesterday's activity. Review "I" Messages, also verbal and nonverbal communication. Have the class brainstorm emotions; write these on chart paper. Sort into a T chart according to positive and negative emotions. Discuss negative emotions as those with the capacity to trigger automatic responses before one can decide how to respond. Write the word *responsibility* on the board. Separate this word into parts; state that *responsibility* is one's ability to respond. You might then do one of the following activities:

♦ Write a situation that would cause someone to feel a particular emotion; have students guess that emotion.

♦ Have students act out emotions nonverbally for the class to guess.

♦ Have each student choose an emotion, then cut images from magazines to create a collage depicting that emotion.

♦ Ask students to create a poem, song, rap song, and so on, illustrating specific emotions.

Close by discussing why it is important to identify emotions and how to develop strategies to deal with negative feelings. Brainstorm how this could enhance their lives now and in the future.

Homework, Cleanup, PE, Closing, Dismissal

Day 10

Opening and Sentence Corrections

Literacy

Continue with the same literature as before or start a new short story. Use the modified Reciprocal Teaching Process. Using the overhead projector, model how you wish the recording to be done; share positive examples from yesterday's work. Follow the recording by having students fill out the attitude survey from Chapter 2, What I Think About Writing.

Recess

SSR

Writer's Workshop

Model writing the cover, title page, and "About the Author" segments of the writing project. Use different books for modeling what should be included and how different authors perform this task. You might create an About the Author form to be pasted into the back cover. Use construction paper for covers, and if your school has a spiral-binding machine, use that for binding the books.

Next week, have students self-assess their stories using the Writing Expectations found in Chapter 2. Have them set a writing goal to refer to for the next writing assignment. After scoring the stories with the Writing Expectations rubric, share your assessments with students. Collect prewrites and first drafts, staple to the rubric scores, and place in students' portfolios. Next week, allow fifteen to twenty minutes per day for Author's Chair, so students can read and share their final work. Display books for them to read during SSR. Add the completed books to portfolios for parent conferences.

Math Warm-Ups and Math

Give students a pretest covering the first chapter of the math text to be addressed. Usually, in intermediate grades, revisiting place value, rounding or estimating, greater than/less than, and regrouping are appropriate starting points. If your district uses materials other than textbooks, assess students' prior knowledge using the best available method. Assessments help develop your next unit and reveal modifications needed in your instruction.

Lunch

Read Aloud

Social Studies

Use the Group Definition of Cooperation and Cooperative Triangles activities described in Chapter 5 to reinforce cooperative behaviors. Close this unit on Getting to Know You by reflecting with your students about what they have learned.

Homework, Cleanup, PE, Closure, Dismissal

5

Activities for the First Month

This chapter provides over fifty tried-and-true activities that will build a sense of community in your classroom, encouraging students to get to know one another better. These activities are designed to foster pride and build self-esteem, and some are provided in English and Spanish. They also allow you to get to know who your students are and what they bring to your classroom. These activities cover the range of skills from reading, writing, math, and social studies to suggestions for homework activities and "sponge" activities that soak up time to keep students busy as they are waiting for others to finish a task.

COMMUNITY BUILDER ACTIVITIES

Appreciation Words

> *Materials*: Paper, pencils, chart paper (optional)
> *Grouping*: Whole class and teams
> *Approximate Time*: 20–30 minutes

Directions:

1. Choose one child for demonstration purposes, and write a list of six to ten words describing that person. Use words that describe his or her special attributes, such as *caring, helpful, a good listener, friendly, good at sports, creative, thoughtful,* and *contributes to class discussions.* Review the procedures for teacher-led discussion.

2. Have the class guess who the person might be. Write each guess on the board.

3. After several guesses, tell the class that all their guesses are right in a way, because all of the people they guessed have these characteristics.

4. Tell them the name of the person you thought of when making the list.

5. As a class or in teams, brainstorm words of appreciation. It might help if you ask the students to think about particular people. Younger students could think about characters from a book you have read to them. Make a list from the students' suggestions and display it in the room.

Extension: Throughout the year, have the class develop a list of appreciation words for a special student. Record the words on chart paper for the student to take home at the end of the week. Students may also sign the chart or write personal comments and compliments on it before it is taken home. Periodically, discuss words from the list (their meanings, the type of things a person would do to exhibit a particular attribute, and so on), and add a couple of the words to your regular spelling list.

Characteristics: Following is a list of words that might help you with this activity if the class gets stuck. You might also give students the task of alphabetizing these words.

friendly	polite	energetic
helpful	eager	outgoing
responsible	enthusiastic	courageous
reliable	fair	resourceful
generous	cheerful	willing
thoughtful	loyal	organized
caring	flexible	compassionate
humorous	creative	considerate

A list of Spanish words may also be useful:

amistoso	considerado	selectivo
agradable	cortés	amable
compasivo	vigoroso	responsable
productivo	inspirado	hábil
generoso	flexible	entusiasta
beneficioso	enérgico	alegre
intrépido	interesante	puntual
inventivo	deseoso	estudioso
justo	comprensivo	capaz

Bingo

Materials: Enough Bingo game sheets for all students (see following page), all students' names written on separate pieces of paper, a bag or other container to put the names in, "prizes"

Grouping: Whole class
Approximate Time: 20–30 minutes

Directions:

1. Have paper monitors pass out the Bingo sheets.

2. Explain the directions and your behavioral expectations. Tell the students, "This activity is a fun way to learn your classmates' names. At the signal, write one name in each box on the Bingo sheet. Do not use any name twice. Try to write as many names as you can from memory. You may use your own name. Then, I will pull a name from this bag. If you have that name on your Bingo sheet, cross it off. When you have five names crossed off in a row, vertically, horizontally, or diagonally, say 'Bingo.'

3. Check for the students' understanding of the directions, then give the signal to start.

4. Circulate around the room to prompt students. They should be able to fill in the names on their sheets in five to ten minutes, depending on the grade level. For younger students, (a) make a game board with fewer boxes, (b) write students' names so that they just need to recognize the beginning sounds, and (c) have students work in pairs.

5. Give your zero-noise signal and repeat the procedure again if the students begin to call out during the game.

6. Play until someone says, "Bingo." Verify the names he or she has crossed out with the names you have pulled out of the bag. Continue play until another student has Bingo. Repeat until several students "win."

7. Give out prizes of graham crackers, raisins, popcorn, or the like. Be sure everyone gets a prize. You might want to give the "winners" a little more. This game is good to play right before recess, so the students can be excused as soon as they get their snacks.

Figure 5.1   Bingo Grid

BINGO

		FREE		

Conflict Resolution: "I" Messages

Materials: None
Grouping: Cooperative groups of four
Approximate time: 60 minutes

Directions:

1. Tell your students you will all be working on skits in which they'll be practicing "I" messages. Give sample "I" messages, such as, "I can't think with a lot of noise."

2. Act out the following skit for the class:

   First person: Jane's hogging the ball. She won't let me play.

   Second person: You're too dumb to play. You don't even know how to play the game. You're a tattletale. (Runs off to join other friends.)

3. Talk about what happened and the kind of message it was. ("You" message, blaming, didn't tell how they felt or what they needed from the other person. No compromise happened.)

4. Ask what could have been said instead. Ask, "How can we give better 'I' messages?" Generate ideas. Have two students act out a better way to resolve the conflict.

5. Generate a list of things that make students angry. List them on the board.

6. Divide the class into groups of four. Tell them that each group needs to create a skit in which one person gets angry at another. Two students from the group will act out the skit with "you" messages, and then the other two students will reenact the skit with "I" messages and compromise.

7. Explain procedures—where you want students to work, the acceptable noise level, and so on. Discuss how the groups might choose the characters for their skits fairly. Give the groups ten to fifteen minutes to work on their skits.

8. Bring the students back to their seats and have each group perform its two skits.

Closure: Ask, "What did the groups do differently in the second skits? What did you learn today about resolving conflicts? How can practicing this help our class?"

The Garfunkle Story (Grades K–2)

Materials: One large basic paper doll made of construction paper
Grouping: Whole class
Approximate Time: 20 minutes

Directions:

1. Hold up the paper doll in front of the class and introduce him as Garfunkle. Explain a very tough day in his life: He got up late, his mother yelled at him, he spilled his breakfast, he missed his bus or got a bus citation, and on and on, using examples the kids can relate to in your school. It is particularly good to use things you have seen happen in the class. With each negative incident, fold in a little part of Garfunkle's body to make the doll shorter, and explain how he felt bad and that made him feel smaller. Keep folding in the parts as he gets smaller and smaller. Have him do something such as tease someone or hit someone to try to feel bigger, but instead he gets in trouble and feels even smaller. When you get to the end of your story, Garfunkle should be all folded up.

2. Talk with the class about how it feels at times like that. Ask how many of them have felt that way at times. Brainstorm ways that the kids in Garfunkle's class could make him feel better. Write them on the board.

3. Continue the story, using the ideas the class came up with, opening up Garfunkle with each positive experience until he is whole again. Talk about how you have Garfunkles in the class every day.

Closure: Ask, "How can this story help make our class better?"

Follow-Up: Copy the brainstormed list and post it with Garfunkle to remind students of the kinds of things they can do to help each other feel good and whole.

Group Definition of Cooperation

Materials: Large pieces of paper, crayons or markers, writing paper, pencils
Grouping: Cooperative groups of 3 or 4
Approximate Time: 45–60 minutes

Directions:

1. Students in cooperative groups number off 1 to 3 or 1 to 4, depending on group size. Give each number a job: recorder, reporter, timekeeper, "gopher" (the recorder writes down the group's ideas and final definition, the reporter reports the group's ideas to the class, the timekeeper keeps track of the group's five minutes for discussion, and the gopher gets the paper and pencils the group needs).

2. Tell students that each group will be coming up with a definition of cooperation. All group members must participate and come to consensus on the definition.

3. Give each group a large piece of paper to draw a mural that reflects the group's definition. Discuss cooperation and involvement of every student in the group. Give approximately thirty minutes for the drawing.

4. Have the reporters share their groups' definitions of cooperation and their murals.

Closure: Ask students, "How will cooperation help our class this year? What kinds of things can students do to show cooperation? What does cooperation look like and sound like?" Ask each student to tell his or her group one thing he or she liked about the way the group worked today, or have individual students write or tell one thing they liked about their own behavior and one thing they can improve.

Group Definition of Cooperation: Extensions for Younger Students

♦ *Option 1*: Start with a drawing on butcher paper. Cut into enough puzzle pieces for each student to have a piece, or glue a poster on oak tag and cut into puzzle pieces.

♦ *Option 2*: Purchase a large floor puzzle with enough pieces for everyone in the class. Have the students sit in a circle with their puzzle pieces. Review procedure for putting the pieces together.

♦ *Option 3*: Cut a large piece of butcher paper into puzzle pieces, one for each student. Have students draw something about themselves on their puzzle piece. Put this together for a perfect fit!

Follow the puzzle completion with a brief discussion on how all students cooperated in making the complete picture.

Names Activities

Names is a start-of-the year, shared-writing activity for kindergarten and first grade, although it can be adapted for higher grades. Names teaches the names and sounds of upper and lower case letters, concepts about print (how and why letters go together to create words, sound and spelling in correspondence, and how to recognize patterns, similarities, and differences in print features).

Procedure for Names Activity: First, select one child as *student of the day*. That student's name will progress through the following steps:

1. In advance, write the chosen name on a long strip of paper—one that can be stapled to form a crown worn by the student of the day.

2. On a tagboard strip, slowly write the name while saying the letters aloud. Tape to chart paper.

3. Count the letters in the name with the whole group.

4. Repeat the name. Chant the letters while clapping on each one.

5. Discuss the capital letter.

6. Write the name on the chart paper; have students chant the spelling as you write.

7. Remove the tagboard name card from chart paper. Have students watch as you cut apart each letter. Mix up all letters in a pocket chart.

8. Invite several students to rearrange the letters to form the name.

9. Invite the class to chant the letters. Have them check to see if the name is in the correct order. Slide your finger under each letter to guide chanting.

10. Discuss the name. Focus on concepts about print (e.g., how the name begins and ends, the first or last letter, same letters, different letters, a long or short name, etc.).

11. Interview the student and write a chart story about her or him. Model and think aloud about writing and how mechanics are used when writing.

12. Work the text. (See Morning Message for ideas.)

13. At writing tables, have students write or draw a picture for the student of the day.

14. Students share their writing and drawings with the group. You might decide on only five to six students to share each day.

15. Compile children's writing into a book. Send the book home with the student of the day.

16. Leave the name chart story on display for students to reread.

Problem-Solving Skits

Materials: Vignettes of typical group problems (home or school) likely to happen within your students' age group; these should be on index cards (one per group) along with a chart of criteria for skits.
Grouping: Groups of 3 or 4 students, selected randomly
Approximate Time: 45 minutes

Introduction: Ask students, "When you have a disagreement with friends, what do you do? How do you resolve your problems?" Solicit ideas from the group; record them on the board. You may get answers such as, "We talk about it until we agree, or we toss a coin." Accept all reasonable answers.

Instructions: Tell students they will be working within a group to solve a problem. Each group will receive a vignette, or story, that exemplifies a problem. Allow the group ten minutes to brainstorm on solving that problem, and develop a skit to perform in class demonstrating the problem and solution. State that they will be placed in groups, randomly, and must follow several criteria. (Record these on the board, a chart, or overhead):

♦ Everyone must participate in the skit

♦ The skit must show both problem and solution

♦ The solution must be satisfactory to all in the group

◆ If anyone disagrees with the solution, the group must brainstorm until an agreement is reached

Guided practice: Form random groups of three to four students. Number them off and assign student roles of recorder, facilitator, timekeeper, and so on. Check for understanding of roles. Ask how it will look or sound when the group is working cooperatively. Allow fifteen minutes for skit development. Monitor the level of cooperation within groups.

Closure: Ask each group to perform their skit. Allow several compliments from the class regarding solution and performance. Point out specific examples of cooperation within groups as they worked on skit development. Ask how students might apply what they have learned.

Possible Problem-Solving Vignettes

◆ It is a Saturday, and four friends want to get together. However, one wants to see a movie, one wants to go boogie-boarding at the beach, another wants to ride bikes, and the fourth wants to go to the mall. How will you solve this problem so all four friends spend the day together and are happy with their chosen activity?

◆ Four students are playing four-square during recess. One student calls another out. However, that student disagrees and refuses to leave the game. What do you do?

◆ Two friends agree to play together at recess. One person broke his or her agreement and went off to play with others during recess. How can this be resolved?

◆ Three students were playing at recess. A fourth asked to join in, but the others in the group wouldn't let him or her join them. What happens?

◆ The class is taking a math quiz, and a student notices someone copying his or her answers. What does he or she do?

Know Your Classmates

Materials: Enough teacher-made work sheets for all students, pencils
Grouping: Whole class
Approximate Time: 30 minutes

Directions:

1. Make your own work sheet with the blanks shown on pages 140 and 141.

2. Have paper monitors pass out the work sheets.

3. Explain the directions: "To get the answers to these questions, you must walk around the room and talk to every classmate. Being accurate is better than being quick. You will have about twenty minutes." (The amount of time is up to you. Younger students may need more time or fewer questions.)

4. Give the signal to begin. Circulate around the room, helping, encouraging, keeping students on task, praising work completed, or doing a work sheet yourself.

5. Use your zero-noise signal to indicate when time is up. Have everyone return to his or her seat.

6. Go over each question on the work sheet, asking for a show of hands. For example, "Raise your hand if you have more than two pets," or, "Raise your hand if you have more than four pets." Keep asking questions until you find the student with the most pets, and then ask what types of pets he or she has. The objective of this activity is to help students to get to know their classmates and learn about the differences and similarities among them.

Closure: Ask, "Did anyone learn something about a classmate they didn't know before? What?" Be ready to volunteer what you learned about someone or point out a similarity you learned through this activity.

Figure 5.2   Know Your Classmates Sample

Figure 5.3 Know Your Classmates Template

NAMES GAMES

Action Names

Grouping: Whole class
Approximate Time: 45 minutes

Directions:

1. Have students sit in a circle on the floor.

2. Going around the circle, each person gives his or her name with an action for each syllable. For example, Josefina would need four syllables. She would say, "Josefina," and then say it again slowly: "Jo"—hits right knee with right hand; "se"—hits left knee with left hand; "fi"—claps hands; "na"—slaps knees with both hands.

3. Have the whole group repeat the motions, saying the name two times.

4. Then move on to the next person.

Initial Adjectives

Grouping: Cooperative groups
Approximate Time: 30 minutes

Directions:

1. In cooperative groups, come up with an adjective to describe each person that starts with that person's initial; for example, Active Abdul or Jumping Jabar.

2. Have the entire group then create a chant with rhythm motions (clapping, snapping fingers) that includes the names and adjectives of everyone on the team.

3. Have groups simultaneously share their chants.

Name Song

Grouping: Whole class
Approximate Time: Variable

Directions:

Use the basic name song that follows, and create a song with the names of the students in your class.

Shirley Shirley Bo Birley,
Banana Fana Fo Firley
Fe Fi Mo Mirley, Shirley

Name Scramble

Materials: Enough teacher-made work sheets for all students, pencils
Grouping: Whole class at desks
Approximate Time: 20 minutes

Directions:

1. Make a work sheet that shows the first names of all students in uppercase letters, with each name scrambled (e.g., Mary might be YARM). Vary the difficulty by (a) writing the first letter in uppercase and the rest of the name in lowercase, (b) underlining the first letter, and (c) posting a class list for the students to refer to.

2. Explain the directions and behavioral expectations for this activity. Students are to unscramble classmates' names.

3. Pass out the work sheets.

4. While the students work on unscrambling the names, move around the class offering help, listening to conversations, encouraging interactions, and keeping students on task.

5. After fifteen minutes, give your zero-noise signal and have students stop working.

6. Go around the room to "correct" the work sheets. Have one person read the first unscrambled name, then another read the second, and so on. Or do simultaneous sharing, with students calling out their responses. You may have each person whose name has been unscrambled stand up, so students can associate name and face.

Closure: Ask, "Which name was the most difficult to unscramble for you and why?" Also ask, "Why would I want you to do an activity like this?" Last, ask, "Who can go around the room and name each person?"

Name Scramble 2

Materials: Pencils, scratch paper, teacher-made name strips printed on tagboard with the letters cut apart
Grouping: Whole class at desks, then pairs of students
Approximate Time: 45–60 minutes

Directions:

1. Put the cut-up letter pieces for each name in an envelope—one for each name. (To vary the difficulty of this activity, make the pieces larger by cutting between every other letter; make the cuts distinctive, giving visual clues; or place dots on the backs of pieces for last names.)

2. Explain the directions to the class, including behavioral expectations. Students are to reassemble their classmates' names.

3. Randomly distribute the envelopes, making sure that no one receives his or her own name.

4. At your signal, have each student empty his or her envelope and begin to unscramble the mystery name.

5. Once a student completes the unscrambling task, he or she should find the person whose name is on the strip and "interview" him or her.

6. Using their own interview questions (see the following pages for a sample list in English and Spanish), interviewers must learn five interesting facts that they will use to introduce the person to the class.

7. Wander around the room to keep everyone on task and to listen to conversations.

8. As the students finish, have them check with you to be sure they have completed all parts of the activity. If they have, tell them to write the unscrambled names of the persons they interviewed on the chalkboard. Use this list for the order of introductions. These eight steps should take approximately twenty minutes.

9. Have the students sit at their desks or in a class meeting circle for the introductions.

10. As the students introduce each other, listen for and note particularly good questions.

Closure:

1. Discuss the questions and the type of information you would want to know about someone (for instance, "What was one question you thought was particularly good? Why did you like that one? What type of questions help us know more about the person? If you could pick only five questions, which ones would you pick?").

2. Record the best questions to use as a guide for later in the year to get to know new students.

3. You might want to videotape or tape-record the introductions to play back at the end of the school year.

Introducing . . .

_____
(your partner's name)

Ask your partner each question and record his or her comment.

- ◆ Who are the members in your family?
- ◆ What does your family like to do together?
- ◆ What is something you like to do?
- ◆ Where is your favorite place? Why is it so special?
- ◆ What was the best thing about the summer?
- ◆ I know it's going to be a great school year because
- ◆ One thing I hope we learn about this year is

Presentando . . .

_____
(nombre de tu pareja)

Hazle estas preguntas a tu pareja y apunta sus respuestas.

- ◆ ¿Quiénes son los miembros de tu familia?
- ◆ ¿Qué le gusta a tu familia hacer todos juntos?
- ◆ ¿Qué es algo que te gusta hacer?
- ◆ ¿Cuál es tu lugar preferido? ¿Por qué te es tan especial?
- ◆ ¿Cuál fue lo mejor de tu verano?
- ◆ Sé que va ser un gran año escolar porque
- ◆ Una cosa que espero que aprendamos este año es

Please/Please Don't

Materials: Two pieces of chart paper, markers
Grouping: Whole class

Directions:

1. At the first class meeting, talk with students about the need to come to consensus (agreement) on "how we want to be treated in this classroom."

2. Discuss the process of brainstorming; emphasize the importance of accepting all ideas, with no put-downs or judgments.

3. Question students about why it is important not to judge or put down others' ideas.

4. Set up two charts, one labeled "Please . . ." and the other "Please Don't . . ."

5. Ask students to generate endings to these two requests (think about whether you want them to yell out or raise their hands beforehand, and explain your chosen procedure before beginning).

6. Discuss the students' comments, as appropriate.

7. Reread the charts at the end of the activity.

Closure: Ask, "Why was it important to talk about this together? What can you do to help your classmates feel safe and comfortable here?"

Please/Please Don't : Day 2

Directions:

1. From looking at the lists made the first day, come up with four to six rules that would incorporate all of the students' concerns. These rules should be (a) stated in positive terms, (b) broad enough to cover all general behaviors, and (c) stated simply.

2. Transfer the lists that were generated the day before to the board. Explain to the class that you looked at their lists and could see some rules that seemed to cover all of their requests.

3. Write the rules on the board with a lot of space between them. Tell the students that you want to be sure all of their concerns are covered, so you are going to go through their lists together and decide which rule each item would go under.

4. Read the requests on the lists one by one and have the students tell you which rule to put each under. Allow discussion and negotiation. Keep going until all the requests have been covered.

5. Discuss what to do when someone does something on the "Please Don't" list. Have students brainstorm a list of consequences and grade them from mild to severe. Use these rules as guidelines for the class.

Brainstorming: Cheerios

Materials: One box of Cheerios, felt pens, crayons, one piece of butcher paper per group (20 x 30 inches)

Grouping: Cooperative groups of four

Approximate time: 90 minutes

Directions:

1. Tell the class that this is an activity that will exercise their creative thinking.

2. Divide the class into groups of four, and then have each group number off, 1 through 4. Assign each number a job: recorder, reporter, timekeeper, and gopher. (Write these on the board for reference.)

3. Talk about what brainstorming is—accepting all ideas, no judgments. Then, tell students they will be working on a creative art activity with Cheerios. First they will brainstorm uses for Cheerios, and then they will do an art project substituting Cheerios for objects in the picture.

4. Have the student groups brainstorm lists of possible uses for Cheerios in a picture (rings, necklaces, wheels for cars, and so on). The group gophers get paper, and the recorders write their groups' ideas. The timekeepers allow five minutes for the task.

5. Have the reporters come up front to share five of their groups' ideas. Record these ideas on the board for later use in the art project.

6. Now, have the groups work on an art project cooperatively. They will need to decide on a scene and what each person will be responsible for drawing. You may give each one a different color pen to be sure they all contribute. Each group will draw a scene, using Cheerios in place of drawn items as much as possible. For example, a car might have Cheerios as tires. Give approximately forty-five minutes for the art project. Gophers distribute Cheerios and butcher paper.

7. Have the groups share and talk about their projects with the class.

Closure: Ask the groups how they decided on their scenes. Ask each group what made its project successful. Ask students within the groups to compliment each other for some specific contributions they made to the project.

Extension: Have the student groups brainstorm analogies (write the words and definitions on the board): "A Cheerio is like a _____ because _____." Talk about the attributes of a Cheerio (shape, size, color, other qualities), and then brainstorm a few analogies as a class. Example: "A Cheerio is like a tire because it's round and has a hole in the middle." Have the recorders report their groups' analogies. Record these on the board.

Partner Drawings

Materials: Colored construction paper, various colors of pastel chalks (two per student)
Grouping: Whole class
Approximate Time: 30–45 minutes

Directions:

1. Have music on quietly in the background.

2. Have students work in partner teams. Make sure each partner has two pieces of chalk and that each partnership has one piece of paper. Tell students they may not talk during the art session.

3. One partner starts by drawing any continuous line and stops. The next partner puts his or her chalk on the paper where the last line ended and draws any continuous line and stops. The work goes back and forth until, through nonverbal communication, the partners decide they are finished.

Closure: Ask students, "What did you enjoy about the process? How did you and your partner decide when you were finished? How did you feel about your drawings?"

Variation: Both partners hold one piece of chalk together and create together, still with no talking. For closure on this activity, ask students, "Who was the leader? Did the leadership change? How did you feel?"

Shields

Materials: A shield for each student (make copies of the black-line master on the next page and copy onto 8 x 11-inch tagboard or construction paper for final copy), felt pens, crayons
Grouping: Individuals
Approximate Time: 45–60 minutes

Directions:

1. Find some pictures of coats of arms or family shields in an encyclopedia. Show these to your students, and tell them that the pictures or emblems in the sections of these shields represent things about that family.

2. Tell students that today they will be making their own shields. They will be getting a shield outline and will need to draw a picture and write a caption in each section. Today, they will be making a practice copy, and tomorrow they will make the final one.

3. Draw a shield on the board and write a label in each section (see the sample on the next page). Students will fill in the shields with pictures or statements (or pictures with captions for each label).

4. Check for understanding, and then have paper monitors pass out the shield blanks. Circulate as the students begin, to be sure they understand what they should be doing.

Closure: Tell the students you will look over their shields that night, help with editing, and return them tomorrow so they can make their final copies. Ask, "Why are family shields important? Did you realize something special about your family as you did this?"

Shields: Day 2

Directions:

Return the practice shields and allow time for students to make their final shields on tagboard or white construction paper.

Figure 5.4 Shield Sample

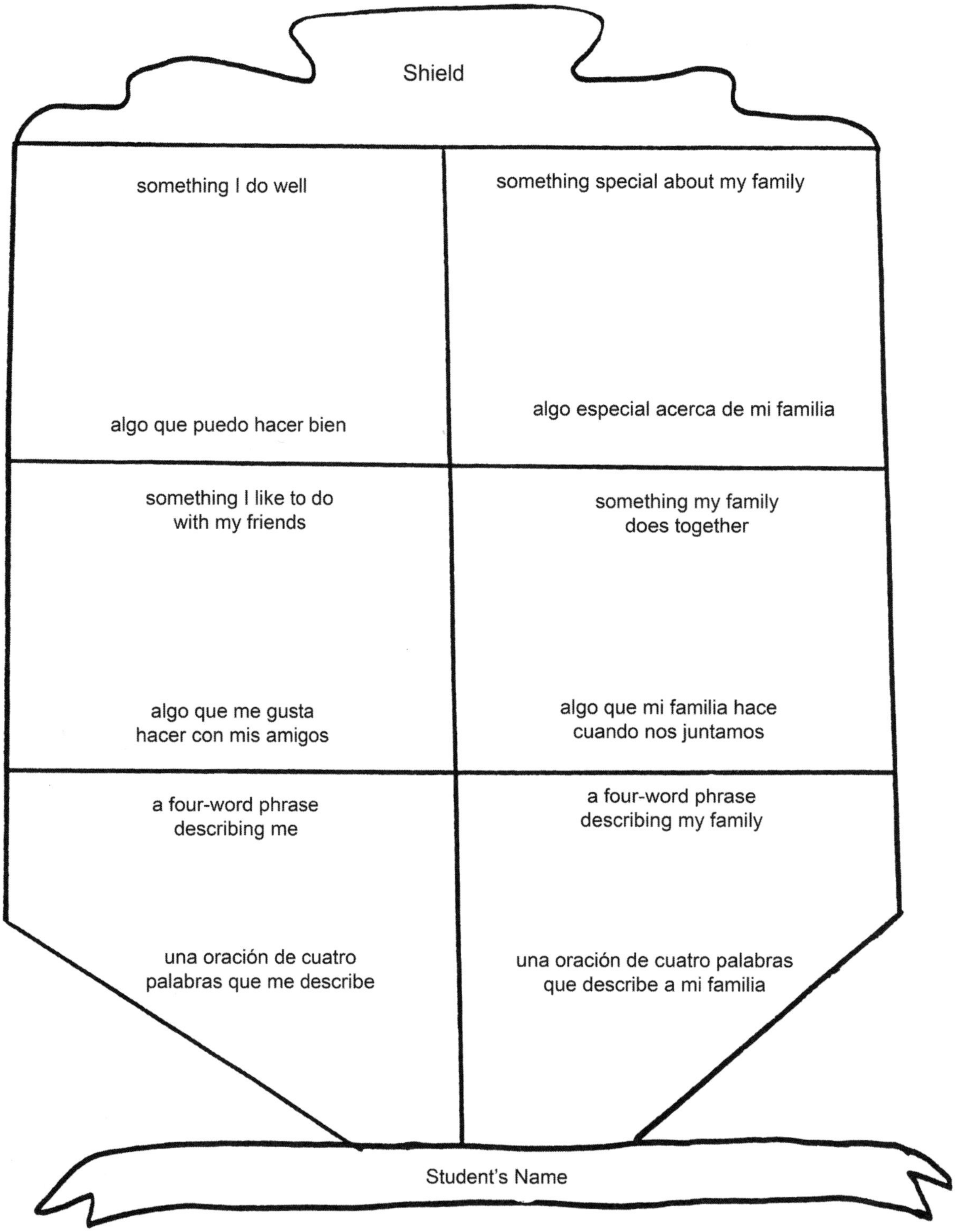

Shield

something I do well

algo que puedo hacer bien

something special about my family

algo especial acerca de mi familia

something I like to do
with my friends

algo que me gusta
hacer con mis amigos

something my family
does together

algo que mi familia hace
cuando nos juntamos

a four-word phrase
describing me

una oración de cuatro
palabras que me describe

a four-word phrase
describing my family

una oración de cuatro palabras
que describe a mi familia

Student's Name

Figure 5.5 Shield Template

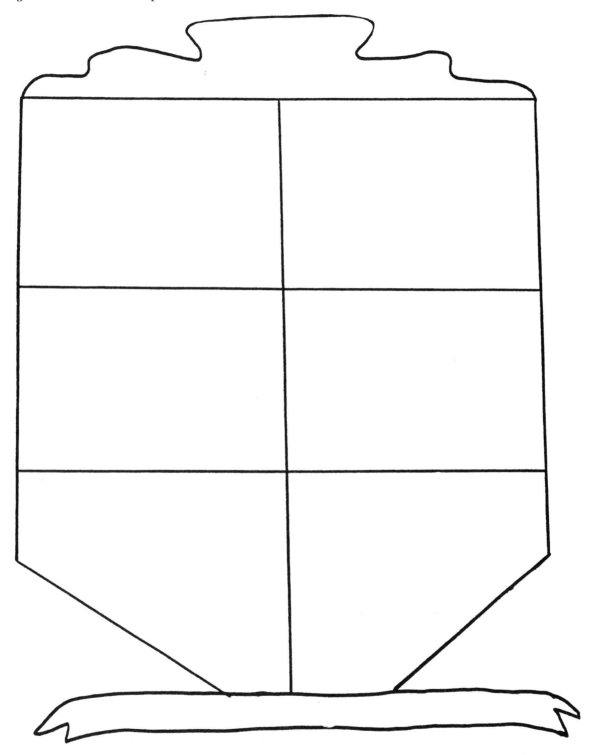

Find Someone Who . . .

Materials: Enough work sheets for all students, pencils
Grouping: Independent, whole class
Approximate Time: 40 minutes

Directions:

1. Have students put their names on the tops of their work sheets, and then go over the "Someone Who" statements orally so everyone can read them.

2. Have students get as many people as possible to sign their names by the statements that apply to them. Students must ask, "Do you . . .?" or "Have you ever . . .?" before someone can sign their papers. (This is an activity to build language skills as well as get to know one another.)

3. Tell students, "You may sign someone else's paper only once, and others can sign your paper only once each." Review the signal to stop.

4. Call time when a few students are close to finishing their pages.

Closure: Discuss who signed for each of the statements. You might want to graph the results. Ask students what they learned about their classmates.

Name _____

Find someone who . . .

Has three brothers _____

Likes tortillas _____

Plays baseball _____

Likes to dance _____

Was born in another country _____

Likes rock music _____

Has read *Ramona the Pest* _____

Eats cereal for breakfast _____

Walks to school _____

Can speak a language other than English _____

Has a cat for a pet _____

Has ridden a horse _____

Has a truck in the family _____

Has a baby in the family _____

Has long hair _____

Has a fireplace in his or her house _____

Nombre _____

Encuentra a alguien que . . .

Tenga tres hermanos _____

Le gusten las tortillas _____

Juegue a béisbol _____

Le guste bailar _____

Nació en otro país _____

Le guste la música rock _____

Haya leído *Ramona la Chinche* _____

Coma cereales para el desayuno _____

Venga caminando a la escuela _____

Pueda hablar otro idioma además del inglés _____

Tenga un gato como mascota _____

Haya montado al caballo _____

Tenga un camión en su familia _____

Tenga un bebé en su familia _____

Tenga el cabello largo _____

Tenga una chimenea en su casa _____

LANGUAGE ARTS ACTIVITIES

Interactive Writing: Interactive Journals

Preparation: Prepare journals for each child. Staple twenty to thirty sheets of writing paper into construction-paper covers—or use three-prong report covers, if available.

Introducing Interactive Journals: Demonstrate the following process several times before your class. If possible, demonstrate with another adult (have one person play the student's role). If not, use several students.

Procedure:

1. Student writes or draws on one page of her or his journal.

2. Student "reads" journal entry to teacher.

3. Teacher responds to entry orally, engaging the child in conversation.

4. Teacher responds to the entry in written form—as a comment or question—then models writing, slowing speech to match the writing.

5. Teacher invites student to read the response.

6. Teacher mediates (scaffolds) the student's attempts to write a response.

Considerations:

♦ Interact and respond to each entry. Do not ask students to write in their journals if you cannot respond.

♦ Provide immediate response and scaffolding for emergent writers. Their writing and message will not "carry" over time.

♦ Respond to content before mechanics, or students may become reluctant risk takers.

♦ Do not provide prompts. The student's writing comes from within and should express his or her own voice. Work with a student who has difficulty finding a topic. Brainstorm or engage in conversation about her or his life and interests.

♦ Scaffolding is individualized. The key teaching points evolve from student's developmental writing stages.

♦ Journal entries provide a developmental history of a child's writing. Put copies of these entries (over time and place) into the student's portfolio. These samples communicate progress to parents and provide ideas on how their child maybe helped at home.

Shared Writing

Morning Message

This is a shared writing activity. The teacher models writing while showing students the relationship between the spoken and written words. Specific mechanics or concepts about print are explicitly explained and modeled.

Keep your messages brief at the start of school year. Create messages that build your classroom community and are relevant to students' lives and experiences (e.g., in Room 2, we are learning about how to cooperate). Vary these messages: Include fact, fiction, rhymes, questions, exclamations, and letter writing.

Crucial to implementing this strategy is the metacognition a teacher demonstrates to her or his class, talking through thinking. Follow this process:

1. Appear to think about what you might write. Discuss your various ideas.

2. Write a message. Think aloud as you write; discuss each aspect of your writing (e.g., "When I start to write a sentence, I must remember to use a capital letter").

3. Have students read the message as you write (include rereading from the beginning). You are now modeling the process that writers use when they recapture beginning thoughts and ideas, before completing their piece.

4. On completion of your message, guide students in rereading it fluently.

5. Work the text by asking children to identify and mark various concepts about print and mechanics. (See the following section.)

6. Soon after Morning Message, students should have an opportunity to write independently, either in a Morning Message Journal or an Interactive Journal or by becoming involved in Writer's Workshop.

Working the Text

Have students circle, underline, or in some way mark these aspects of text:

♦ Capital letters
♦ Rhyming words
♦ Words beginning with the same letter
♦ Punctuation
♦ Spaces between words
♦ Words with the same sound
♦ Upper and lower case differences
♦ Little words inside big words: "mar" is inside "mariposa;" "he" is inside "she"
♦ Words that are the same
♦ Names

- Number of words in a sentence
- Number of sentences
- *Where* to start writing; *where* to proceed after getting to the end of a line

Journals (Grades 2–6)

Build on your students' interests, hobbies, experiences, and family backgrounds with journal prompts. Invite them to write about subjects or places they would like to explore. Weave in informational facts from their community and the world that might interest them or affect their lives:

Journal Prompts

- If you had all the time in the world, where would you travel?
- If you were a famous athlete, what sport would you play? What would your life be like?
- It's a sunny Saturday, and you and your friends _____.
- Yesterday, the local skateboard park was closed indefinitely due to a serious injury. How do you feel about that? What do you think should happen as a result?
- If you could take only three people with you on a trip around the world, who would you choose? Why?
- What are the qualities of a great teacher?
- What are the ingredients for a perfect summer?
- When you can't fall asleep, what do you think about?
- What is something that makes you feel happy?
- What is something that you find scary?
- What kind of animal would you like to be?
- What makes you feel frustrated?
- What makes you laugh?
- If you were lost in the woods and it got dark, what would you do?
- What do you think you might be doing in twenty-five years?
- What are your best qualities?

Sentence Corrections

Sentence corrections can be a daily transition activity but should be followed by mini-lessons on the mechanics of writing.

Materials: Sentence Corrections Journal or a specific tab in student binder; pencils, two sentences written incorrectly on the board or transparency, answer key

Grouping: Individual

Approximate Time: Weekly mini-lesson: 20 minutes; daily practice: 10–15 minutes

Introduction: Prior to the lesson, assess student writing to determine the kinds of errors they are making. Design a lesson for the whole class or small groups, depending on the need. Provide mini-lessons showing run-on sentences, fragments, use of capitalization, or other needed skills. Follow with daily opportunities for students to practice their skills by correcting sentences on the board.

Instructions: After students come in from recess, have them copy the two sentences into their journal (or binder paper), making the appropriate corrections as they write. Be clear on what they should do when work has been completed.

Guided practice: Correct the two sentences with your students. Invite a volunteer to come to the board (or overhead) and make the first revision. Always ask for an explanation of the student's thinking, such as: "What rule were you following?" or "How did you know to make that change?" If the revision is incorrect, ask, "Does anyone have another idea for this revision?" Again, ask for student thinking concerning the change. Let them know the correct answer, then ask them to make the change in their entry. Continue until all necessary changes have been made.

Closure: Ask students to write (or describe to a partner) what they learned in terms of grammar, spelling, or mechanics. Allow a few minutes for whole-group sharing. Periodically, have students write their goals for Sentence Corrections. Check back in a week or so for personal reflection and assessment of progress.

Ideas for Mini-Lessons

Instructions: Teach each of these skills within context. Model the concepts by thinking aloud during Morning Message. Also, request contributions from students.

- Using capital letters to start sentences
- Using capital letters for proper nouns
- Using periods
- Using question marks
- Using exclamation marks
- Using quotation marks
- Using possessives ('s)
- Using apostrophes with contractions
- Using plurals
- Using "-ed" endings
- Using commas to separate items in a series
- Using commas in the greeting and closing of a letter
- Using colons
- Using semicolons
- Using parentheses
- Run-on sentences
- Homonyms

Letters

Materials: Writing paper, pencils, enough teacher-written letters for all students, an envelope for each letter

Grouping: Whole class, individual

Approximate Time: 20–30 minutes

Directions:

1. Before this class session, write a letter, leaving the name of the addressee blank. Make it friendly and chatty. In the letter, tell about yourself, what you like, your hobbies, and so on. You could include major units you have planned and ask for students' thoughts about school. At the end of the letter, ask them to write back to you, telling about themselves. Make enough copies for all your students. Before delivering the letters, address them individually with the students' names and put them in envelopes, also addressed individually.

2. Pass out the letters. Generally, students' curiosity is piqued by this, and they begin without a lot of direction. If they do not begin working silently after two to three minutes, remind them of the procedures for independent work. Tell them they will have about twenty minutes to write their letters (this will vary with the grade level of the class). Tell them what they may do if they finish early (read a book, do a special work sheet you have ready, etc.). Circulate to keep students on task and to encourage those who have a hard time starting.

3. When you see that everyone has finished, collect the letters and express your interest in reading them. (Save the letters to use in your student assessments; see Chapter 6.)

Quotation Discussion

Materials: A meaningful quotation, paper, pencils

Grouping: Variable (groups of four, individual, or whole class)

Directions:

1. Write a meaningful quotation on the board.

2. Ask students to discuss what the quotation means in cooperative groups.

3. Ask individuals to write down the quotation, tell what it means, and give personal examples of how the quotation applies to their own lives.

4. Form a large circle and discuss what the quotation means (no judgments) to different people.

Closure: Ask the class, "What did you learn from this discussion?"

Extensions: This can be used as a homework assignment. Ask students to discuss the quotation at home, at the dinner table, and report back.

Famous Quotations

"Whether you think you can or think you can't—you are right."

Henry Ford

"If it is to be . . . It is up to me."

William Johnson

"Everyone has a fair turn to be as great as he pleases."

Jeremy Collier

"No one can make you feel inferior without your permission."

Eleanor Roosevelt

"It's not so much what you do that makes you special . . . It's who you are."

Anonymous

"Every job is a self-portrait of the person who did it. Autograph your work with excellence."

Anonymous

"The secret to success in any human endeavor is concentration."

Kurt Vonnegut

"Nothing great was ever achieved without enthusiasm."

Ralph Waldo Emerson

"If you're not part of the solution, you're part of the problem."

M. Scott Peck

Dichos Famosos

"Si crees que puedes o si crees que no puedes—tienes razón."

Henry Ford

"Si se va a lograr . . . depende de mi."

William Johnson

"No es tanto lo que haces que te hace especial, sino quien eres."

Anónimo

"El secreto del éxito en cualquier empeño humano es la concentración."

Kurt Vonnegut

"Sin entusiasmo, ninguno de los grandes hechos se hubieran llevado a cabo."

Ralph Waldo Emerson

"Si no eres parte de la solución, eres parte del problema."

M. Scott Peck

"El respeto al derecho ajeno, es la paz."

Benito Juarez

Wiggly Line Drawing

Materials: Enough work sheets for all students, pencils or crayons
Grouping: Independent
Approximate Time: 45 minutes

Directions:

1. Place Wiggly Line work sheets and pencils or crayons on desks so that when students come in, they can do this as a transition activity.

2. Tell students to look at the work sheet and follow the instructions. As they are working, roam around the class to answer any questions and provide encouragement. Note anyone having trouble reading the directions or getting started writing.

3. As students finish their work, be ready to put all of the work sheets directly up on the wall as a display of their drawing and writing.

4. Look at the writing samples to note where each student is developmentally in his or her writing skills. Save these samples to use in one of your initial assessments.

Closure: Read a few of the Wiggly Line stories to the class each day until they have all been shared. Ask the class to share some things they liked.

*White out several of the writing lines for second and third graders. This will give the students more space for their drawings.

Name _____ Date _____

Wiggly Line/Línea Ondulada

Use this line to begin a picture. Then write a story about your picture.

Utiliza esta línea para comenzar un dibujo. Escribe un cuento sobre su dibujo.

_____

_____

_____

_____

_____

_____

_____

_____

_____

_____

_____

_____

_____

_____

MATH ACTIVITIES

Monthly Calendar Lesson

The following calendar grid(s) can be used each month as a directed lesson on calendar skills and number writing. Sending a calendar home each month with an art project and poem or song that reflect your theme is an easy and effective way to communicate with parents.

Materials: Calendar grids (on the following pages), construction paper
Grouping: Small groups or entire class

Preparation:

- ◆ *For kindergarten*: Write the month and year and fill in the dates above the number 10 at the beginning of the year. Duplicate a copy for each child plus an extra for yourself.

- ◆ *For First Grade*: Leave all dates blank. Duplicate a copy for each child plus an extra for an overhead transparency if you plan to do the lesson with the whole class.

- ◆ Staple a copy of the calendar grid to the bottom of a 12 x 18-inch piece of construction paper.

- ◆ Plan and duplicate a simple art project that represents what you will be studying that month. You may also wish to duplicate a reduced version of a song or poem that the children are learning.

Procedure:

1. The first time you do the calendar, you will want to do a directed lesson. Model writing each number, then ask the children to write the number. For first grade, you may wish to model writing a series of numbers, then have children write them.

2. Model how to complete the art project before you ask children to do it independently.

Follow-up ideas:

- ◆ Send the calendar home, with instructions on using it, as part of homework. For example, prepare a simple list of questions that children can complete with their parents: How many Tuesdays are there in September? Does anyone in your family have a birthday in September? When?

- ◆ Post the calendar in your classroom. Use it to model how to write important upcoming events at school and in your classroom. Encourage children to use the calendar to count the number of days until an upcoming event, and so on.

Figure 5.6 Monthly Calendar

Monday	Tuesday	Wednesday	Thursday	Friday	Saturday	Sunday

Figure 5.6 Monthly Calendar

Domingo	Lunes	Martes	Miércoles	Jueves	Viernes	Sábado

Math Challenges

Materials: Math journals, pencils
Grouping: Individual
Approximate Time: 15–20 minutes

Directions:

1. Begin the math period with a brief challenge activity. Have a place on the board where the math challenge is written each day, so students can get started when they come in. The challenge might be from any of the math strands, or it might focus on the computational process you are currently teaching. You might want to make up math problems using information that is relevant to your class or that fits in with what you are studying in other content areas (e.g., if you are studying marine life, your problems could be about otters, fish, and so on).

2. Have students work the math challenge problem in their math journals. (See Math Journal activity, described later.)

3. When the time is up, discuss the various strategies students used to solve the problem. Have several students come to the board to share their diagrams and equations and tell about the various strategies they used to solve the problem. Encourage the students to draw pictures to show their solutions and have them write equations to explain their computations.

Examples of Challenges:

1. How much will a dozen 6-cent stamps cost? (12 x \$.06 = \$.72)

2. There are 11 clothespins strung on a line. Each clothespin is 6 centimeters from the previous clothespin. How many centimeters is it from the first clothespin to the last clothespin? (6 x 10 = 60 cm)

3. If eggs cost 96 cents a dozen, how many eggs can you buy for 3 quarters, 2 dimes, and 1 penny? (\$.75 + \$.20 + \$.01 = \$.96; 1 dozen)

4. One place charges \$39.00 a day to rent a car. Another place charges \$58.00 a day. How much can you save by renting the car from the first place rather than the second? (\$58.00 – \$39.00 = \$19.00)

5. Mom has 4 pies. She wants to cut them so each of 8 people has the same size piece. What is the size of each piece? (4 ÷ 8 = 1/2 pie for each piece)

6. Rosa had _____ rose bushes. She went to the garden shop and bought 9 more. How many plants did she have in the beginning if she has 21 in all? (21 – 9 = 12)

7. Estimate how many shoelace holes are in our class today.

8. Apples cost 43 cents a pound. How many pounds of apples did I buy if I spent $2.15? ($2.15 ÷ $.43 = 5 lbs.)

En Español

1. ¿Cuánto cuesta una docena de timbres de 6 centavos?
   (12 x $.06 = $.72)

2. Once pinzas están en la línea. Cada pinza está a 6 centímetros de la otra. ¿Cuántos centímetros hay entre la primera pinza y la última?
   (6 x 10 = 60 cm)

3. Si una docena de huevos cuesta 96 centavos, ¿Cuántos huevos puedes comprar con 3 "quarters," 2 "dimes," y 1 centavo?
   ($.75 + $.20 + $.01 = $.96; 1 docena)

4. En un lugar cobran $39.00 al día por rentar un carro. En otro lugar cobran $58.00 al día. ¿Cuánto puedes ahorrar si rentas el carro en el primer lugar en vez del segundo lugar? ($58.00–$39.00 = $19.00)

5. Una madre tiene 4 pasteles. Ella quiere cortar 8 pedazos para que cada persona tenga pedazos del mismo tamaño. ¿Cuál es el tamaño de cada pedazo? (1/2 pastel para cada uno)

6. Rosa tenía ____ rosales. Ella fue a la jardinería y compró 9 más. ¿Cuántos rosales compró si tenía 21 en total? (21–9 = 12 rosales)

7. ¿Aproximadamente, cuántos agujeros de cordón hay en todos los zapatos en la clase?

8. Las manzanas cuestan 43 centavos la libra. ¿Cuántas libras de manzanas compré hoy si gasté $2.15? ($2.15 ÷ $.43 = 5 lbs.)

The Class Age

Materials: Calculators (if possible, one for every two students)
Grouping: Partners
Approximate Time: 30–40 minutes

Directions:

1. Have each student guess what the sum of everyone's age will be. Record the estimates on the board.

2. Give each set of partners a calculator. If this is their first time with calculators, give students some time to play around with them; let them know what is acceptable and what is not. Go over the functions of the keys and do a couple of practice problems. Also go over the care and handling of a calculator.

3. Review teacher-led lesson procedures.

4. Go around the class, asking each student how old he or she is. Have the partners enter each age in their calculators and then push the plus key. Ask for a subtotal after each entry. If any pair has made an error, they can clear the calculator and start again with the correct subtotal.

5. Compare the results with the estimates.

Extensions:

1. Graph this activity.

2. Do this activity with other attributes, such as the combined heights of class members. Or how long a line would the class make if all the students lay down head to toe? Older students could also find the average, range, and median age, height, etc.

Cooperative Triangles

Materials: Enough copies of the cooperative triangle (see next page) for all students, crayons, pencils, felt pens

Grouping: Cooperative groups of three

Approximate Time: 30 minutes

Directions:

1. Have students work in groups of three to count all the triangles in the figure. Assign group jobs: recorder, reporter, and facilitator (checks for agreement, keeps discussion going, makes sure everyone participates).

2. Each group must come up with a strategy for keeping track of the triangles counted.

3. Give approximately five minutes for the task.

4. Have the reporters share their groups' findings. Have facilitators tell about the strategies their groups used in keeping track of the triangles.

Closure: Come to consensus, if possible. There is no need to tell the answer; some students will pursue the problem.

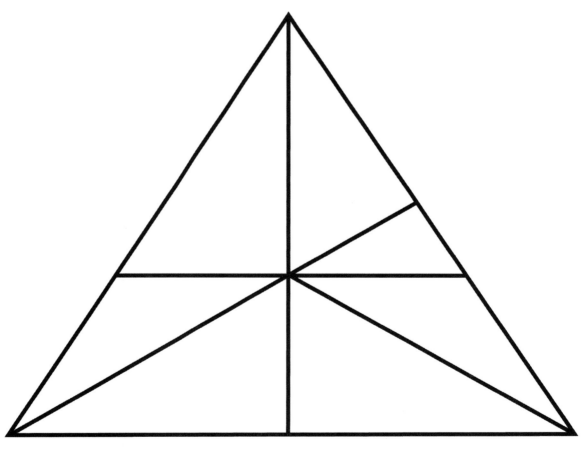

Problem-Solving Strategies: Estimating Raisins

Materials: Construction paper, scrap paper, crayons, felt pens, one half-ounce box of raisins for each cooperative group

Grouping: Cooperative groups of four

Approximate Time: 30 minutes

Directions:

1. Write the following directions on the board:

   a. As a group, estimate how many raisins are in a half-ounce box.

   b. Write the estimate and tell how you came up with it. Recorder writes group's ideas.

   c. Open the box and count how many raisins are in it. Determine a strategy for counting them quickly.

   d. Write the number of actual raisins in your box, and tell the difference between the estimated and actual number of raisins.

   e. Divide the raisins equally among the members of your group.

   f. Draw a picture of each member's share of raisins.

   g. Write an equation or number sentence for dividing the raisins.

2. Explain to the students that they will be working in cooperative groups. Each person will have a role: The gopher will distribute and collect the materials; the recorder will write down what group members say; the leader will make sure everyone participates equally, using positive praise; and the timekeeper will keep the group on task and on time. Assign roles to students by having them number off and making all Number 1s gophers, and so on.

3. Read over the directions written on the board, modeling an example of how the task might be done and reviewing what each of the roles might look like during the process. Review cooperative group procedures with the class.

4. Explain that when the groups finish, they will all have group sheets that explain the process of how they solved the problem. These group sheets will all be put into a class book.

Closure: When their group sheet has been turned in, have each group discuss and write how they divided up the task and what made the group work well.

Evaluation: Gather on the rug and discuss what criteria should be evaluated: neatness, organization, content, correctness, enhancements. Go through all of the group sheets and evaluate them together against the chosen criteria (you might assign ten points to each area). In this way, you will model evaluation for the class for future journal entries. You may graph your results.

Math Journal

Materials: Folders for all students with graph or grid paper stapled inside, pencils.

Grouping: Whole class, individual
Approximate Time: Variable

Directions:

1. Explain to your students that math journals are places where they write about how to solve math problems. They provide students with an opportunity to think through their strategies for solving problems so that they may apply those strategies in other situations. (These journals also provide you with valuable information on students' problem-solving skills. They are a great way to integrate math and writing skills and to develop expository writing skills, as well.)

2. Use the raisin estimation activity to have students begin the process of math journals in a cooperative setting. After the activity, explain that the students' journals will be evaluated in the same way the class book was.

3. Give each student a folder with graph or grid paper stapled inside to use as a math journal. Have the students begin their journals by reflecting on the process of doing math cooperatively in the raisin estimation activity. Ask, "What do you like about doing math cooperatively compared with doing it alone?" Discuss and share some entries from volunteers.

4. Use journals a few times a month as an in-depth project. Have students explain and illustrate the process of solving a problem.

5. Use journals daily to work on or record math challenge problems.

6. Have students use the journals also to record their feelings about math and to create their own math problem stories. Have students reflect on their experience in math and what they have learned or what they are having difficulty with.

Assessment: Collect six to eight journals each week to assess (everyone is assessed monthly). Skim through and make some notes in your anecdotal record log about students' thinking skills (logical, sequential, organizational strategies). Use the criteria the class decided on for evaluation (neatness, content, correctness, enhancements). You may want to photocopy a page or two of each student's journal to keep in his or her math folder to show thinking skills to parents or to show strengths or weaknesses in strategies.

Graphing

Materials: Paper, pencils, pens, graph paper, chart paper
Grouping: Partners
Approximate Time: 45 minutes

Directions:

1. Have the students work in pairs. Pair them up ahead of time: have them count off or let them self-select their partners.

2. Discuss the types of questions the class used in Partner Introductions to get to know their classmates. Record the questions on the board.

3. Have each pair of students select a question, or assign a question to each pair.

4. Let the pairs work together to decide the type of graph they want to make and how they should record the information. Review various types of graphs and have samples of each available. For younger students, decide the type of graph they should use and teach them how to collect the data.

5. Give the class ten minutes to move around the room to get the data for their graphs.

6. Have students return to their seats to begin work on their graphs. Supply pens, graph paper, and chart paper. While the students are working, encourage them to work together and to do their best work on the graphs. Mention some elements of a useful graph: a title, clearly labeled information, legibility, and so on.

7. When the graphs are complete, have each pair write a sentence explaining what their graph says. Display the graphs in the room as a student-made bulletin board.

Extension: Have students create surveys to take home and use to survey five people. Have them create graphs using the new information with their partners the next day.

People Measuring

Materials: Enough pieces of string for all students to have several (cut each piece longer than the tallest student in the class), masking tape, pencils
Grouping: Partners
Approximate Time: 30–40 minutes

Directions:

1. Go over the procedures for a teacher-led lesson with small groups.

2. Have students pair up. You can assign partners ahead of time or have the students number off. The important part is that no one feels left out and that everyone has a partner.

3. Pass out several pieces of string to each student. (Older students could do this activity using meter sticks or tape measures.)

4. First, have the students, in pairs, help each other measure and cut their pieces of string to the exact height of their partners. Then, have them measure each others' arm spans and cut strings to that length. Give the students time to complete the measuring (and recording, for older students) while you circulate. Give them masking tape to label which body part each piece of string represents; have them initial their labels. The students may continue measuring arms, legs, head circumference, and so on in the same way.

5. Have the students graph their findings in one or more of the following ways. Tape all the strings representing height, arm span, and so on along a wall on a piece of masking tape to see all the different lengths, creating a string graph. Have students measure their strings with rulers, convert their measurements from feet and inches to meters and centimeters, and graph the class.

6. Have students look at relationships between height and arm span or height and head circumference, and so on, making predictions and testing them out. Record the results and compare what they find. Have them tell how their measurements compare; for example, "My height is three times the circumference of my head."

OTHER ACTIVITIES

Homework Ideas

Whenever possible, homework should reinforce in-class work or prepare students for a coming lesson. Part of the purpose of homework is to teach study habits at home. It is important to discuss with students how they might set up a routine to get homework done and put in a special place so they will remember to bring it back. There should be a basket near the classroom door for turning in homework. It can be checked in quickly by an instructional aide or a student. Assigning numbers to be placed in the upper left-hand corners of papers, which correspond to a class record list, will facilitate putting papers in order to check off. Send a letter home to parents to inform them of the homework schedule. (See Chapter 7 for a sample.)

Ideas for Homework Assignments

◆ Read silently or to a brother, sister, or parent for thirty minutes (this can be signed off in a notebook by a parent).

- Write a story based on a story starter, such as "The worst day of my life . . ." or "The best party I can imagine . . ."
- Study math facts related to current in-class math work.
- Walk through your house or neighborhood looking for all the things whose names start with a certain letter, particular sounds, particular smells, things using electricity, things that are living, things that come from different countries, and so on.
- Interview family members on different issues.
- Look for all the pictures, television shows, foods, fabrics, colors, and so on that relate to a particular thematic unit coming up in class.
- Survey neighbors, friends, and family to graph the next day.
- Write about or draw who lives in your house, including at least two adjectives about each person.
- Draw the name of a classmate from a hat in class, and write a description of that person to use in a guess who game.
- Write a letter to a relative, a political leader, or a company to bring in for editing and revision.

Sponge Activities

Sponge activities are so named because they soak up time. They should be fun activities that can be done spontaneously, enhancing learning in subtle ways. Ask your class to brainstorm their favorite games from previous years and keep a list. Have students model the games for the rest of the class when you are ready to play. Some ideas they will probably come up with are Around the World, Multiplication Baseball, and Heads-Up 7-Up.

People Sorting

Think of a rule in your mind, such as students with short sleeves. Call students to come and stand next to you in front of the class. Those that follow the rule (who are wearing short sleeves) stand on your right; others stand on your left. Ask the class if they can guess your rule. Any students who think they know the rule must tell you which side they should stand on. Keep sorting students until you think many people know the rule, then ask them to say what they think your rule is. This is very good for vocabulary development (for learning such words as denim, Velcro, collars, pullovers, jewelry, beige).

Lineups

Have the whole class line up around the room in some of the following ways: in order of birth dates, alphabetical order by first or last name, distance they live from the school, farthest point they have ever traveled to, shortest to tallest. For variation, pass out pictures to use for fastest to slowest transportation, biggest to smallest animal, and so on. Ask students to share what they learned during this activity. Ask what other ways they might line up.

Mastermind

Students try to guess a word you are thinking of by guessing letters. They get an X for each right letter in the right place. They get an O for a right letter but in the wrong place, and they get a dash (–) for a wrong letter. They try to use the fewest guesses possible.

Twenty Questions

Have the students try to guess something you are thinking of by asking only yes-or-no questions. They have twenty questions. Teach the students some questioning strategies that start out in broad categories and narrow down, such as "Is it animal, vegetable, or mineral?" (This is a "free" question, and the only non-yes–no question allowed.) If animal, "Is it a reptile?" If no, "Is it a mammal?" If yes, "Does it live on land?" If no, "Does it live in water?" And so on. One variation on this game is to have students guess a number rather than an object. Encourage them to use terms such as *greater than, less than, odd, even, a multiple of, in the 60s.* Another variation uses careers (What's My Line?). Instead of just yes-or-no questions, students can ask, "Would you . . ." questions, with possible answers being "every day," "sometimes," "hardly ever," and "never."

Wonderball

While passing a ball around a circle, the class chants: "The wonderball goes round and round, / to pass it quickly you are bound. / If you're the one to hold it last, / then for you, the game has passed."

The one holding the ball when the chant ends is out. Keep rounds short, so students can get back into the game.

Switch

Two students go out of the room while everyone else changes seats. When the two come back in, they must return misplaced students to their correct desks within three minutes. (Remove student name cards from desks.)

Clap Action

One student goes out of the room, and the rest of the class decides on an action, such as washing hands or touching the chalkboard. The student returns and tries to guess the action by moving to different areas of the room and trying out different movements. The class guides him or her by clapping louder and louder as the student gets closer to the correct task. A variation on this game, You're Hot, has students call out, "You're getting warmer" (moving toward it), or "You're getting colder" (moving away from it) as a student tries to find a hidden object.

Categories

Sitting with the class in a circle, start a rhythm of clapping and hitting knees. Choose a category (for instance, presidents) and say, "Categories, presidents." Then, each person in turn around the circle has to name a president before two rhythm claps have gone by, or they are out. There are many other categories you can use, such as fruits, domestic animals, words beginning with a certain letter, authors, television shows, and adjectives.

Safari

Decide on a category of attributes (in this example, things with four legs) that will be the same about all the things you are taking on an imaginary safari; tell students they can come with you if they bring the correct kinds of items. You say, "I'm going on a safari and I'm taking an elephant and a chair." If a student wants to go on safari with you, he or she must say, "I'm going with you, and I'm bringing a table (or a dog, or a something else that has four legs)." Students who name the right kinds of items then get up and stand with you in front of the class. If a student wants to bring the wrong kind of item, you say, "Sorry, you can't come." You can vary this game by using other kinds of trips (picnics, vacations) and by using beginning-letter sounds, two-syllable words, or other attributes of the words rather than the objects.

My Aunt Likes Coffee, But She Doesn't Like Tea

Write a couple of items on the board that follow a pattern. Students have to guess other things that fit into the pattern of something "your aunt" would like. For example, using beginning letter sounds, she might like cookies, cakes, coffee, and camping, but not pies, turnovers, tea, or backpacking. As with Safari, you can vary this game by using different patterns: word-ending sounds, number of syllables, and so on.

Function Machine

Draw a picture of or create a three-dimensional function machine that you can put numbers into and change them to something else. The functions can get more and more complex as students get better at the game. Example: "I put in 3 and out comes 9, I put in 6 and out comes 12. What is the function?" (Add 6.) "I put in a 3 and out comes 10, I put in a 4 and out comes 13, I put in a 5 and out comes 16. What is the function?" (Multiply by 3 and add 1.)

PE Ideas

Think out your procedures for each game. Explain any new games prior to leaving the classroom, using drawings on the chalkboard if necessary. Explain to the class the proper dress for PE—tennis shoes and shorts or pants. Remind students of the attention signal to be used outside. Allow two minutes for students to change and meet the class outside. Set the procedures for choosing teams, if necessary, and remind students about the "no put-down" rule. For team games, either you or team captains should choose equal teams at another time to be ready for PE. Vary the types of activities so that not just the athletically inclined enjoy success at PE time.

Besides the following suggested games, relay races, four square, kickball, softball, soccer, and basketball are old standbys that your students will be wanting to learn.

Steal the Bacon

Create two lines and have them both number off so each student has a number; have the lines stand opposite each other, with some space in between. When you call out a number, those students who have that number run out, steal the "bacon" (chalkboard eraser) from the center, and run back over their lines. The one who makes it first gets a point.

Steal the Basket

This is the same as Steal the Bacon, but the students steal a basketball, dribble, and try to make a basket.

Knots

Divide the class into three groups. Each group forms a circle, shoulder to shoulder, and then each student grabs hands with anyone who is not standing next to him or her. Each student must hold the hands of two different people. When these "knots" are all tied, the groups try to untangle the mess without ever letting go of hands. Students must step over and under, twist and turn, but never drop a hand. If a group comes to a deadlock, the teacher may make one break to help them move on. (This and the next game are from *The New Games Book*, by Andrew Fluegelman.)

The Lap Game

Form a circle with everyone facing in one direction. One person lies down, with knees bent and feet flat on the ground. The next person sits down on the first person's knees, forming an easy-chair "lap" for the next person to sit in. This proceeds around the circle until everyone is sitting on each others' laps. The hard part is hoisting up the person who formed the initial lap to sit on the person behind.

T-Ball

This is a noncompetitive form of baseball, good for young beginners to practice their skills. Set two teams up just as in baseball, but instead of getting outs, each student gets a turn at bat, and then you change sides. There is no pitcher; the ball is placed on a tee for the batter to swing at. Do not keep track of runs—this game is just for fun and practice.

Tag Games

These games are noncompetitive and get the class involved and moving. In such games, the object is to *not* be tagged by the person who is IT. Rather than playing one continuous game where only one student is IT, stop play after seven to ten minutes. Choose someone new to be IT; repeat the game.

Octopus Tag: Designate a play area. Class lines up on one side; then, on your signal, runs to the other side. One or more students may be the Octopus who runs around in the middle, trying to tag runners as they run from one side to the other. When a runner is tagged, that person becomes a Tentacle and tries to tag others. Tentacles cannot move from the place where they were tagged—instead, they reach out as the runners run by.

Freeze Tag: Start with the basic set-up as in Octopus Tag. This time, when the person who is IT tags a runner, the runner freezes where he or she was tagged. Other runners help frozen players by crawling through their legs to unfreeze them so they can continue to play.

Blob Tag: Start as with Octopus Tag. The player who is IT tags runners as they run from one side to another of the area. Now, when someone is tagged, he or she holds hands with the person who is IT and together they run to tag other players. As more are tagged and the blob extends, pairs may break off to continue running after others. Game ends when all players have become part of the blob or when too exhausted to proceed.

Color Tag: Start with basic set-up. Whoever is IT stands in the center and calls out a color. All who are wearing that color walk to the other side. Everyone else runs while the player who is IT tries tagging him or her before they reach the other side. If a player is tagged, he or she remains in that spot, trying to tag other runners as they go by, without moving the position of their feet.

Touch Down: Designate a playing area with one team lined up on one side, the opposing team on the other. Choose one team to huddle, so the opposition cannot see their hands. Place a piece of chalk in one player's hands. All team members should pretend they have the chalk. The chosen team gets ready and lines up. When teacher blows the whistle, both teams run toward each other. Team holding the chalk tries to cross the opposing team's line, while that team tries to prevent them by tagging their players. When a player is tagged, he or she must stop and show what they are holding. If the player holding the chalk is tagged, the play is over with no point scored. If the player with the chalk makes it over the line, that team scores a point. Alternate teams so each has a chance to carry the chalk. This is a fast-paced game!

6

Fingerplays and Songs for Oral Language in English and Spanish

This chapter provides fingerplays in English and Spanish, hand and finger motions that accompany songs and poems meant to capture the attention and focus the energy of young children. Teach children the fingerplays during direct instruction time. Tell students when they see you doing fingerplays they are to join in. When you want the class's attention, begin doing the fingerplays with those around you, others will join in until you have everyone's attention. This chapter also provides inclusion songs to help students feel a part of a community, as well as songs that can be tied into thematic units.

ATTENTION-GETTING FINGERPLAYS

These fingerplays are those you should start when you need the group's attention. Learn at least two or three to use the first week of school, then add one each week. You will find you use them all year.

Good Morning
(sung to the tune of "Are You Sleeping?")

Good morning, good morning.
How are you? How are you?
Very well, thank you.
Very well, thank you.
How are you? How are you?

Buenos Días
Buenos días, buenos días.
¿Cómo está? ¿Cómo está?
Muy bien, gracias.
Muy bien, gracias.
¿Y usted? ¿Y usted?

Open Them, Shut Them
Open them, shut them. [hands]
Open them, shut them.
Give your hands a clap.
Open them, shut them.
Open them, shut them.
Fold them in your lap.

Ábranlas, Ciérrenlas (chant)
Ábranlas, ciérrenlas.
Ábranlas, ciérrenlas.
Pla, pla, pla.
Ábranlas, ciérrenlas.
Ábranlas, ciérrenlas.
Pónganlas acá.

One Little Eye (chant)
One little eye goes wink, wink, wink.
Two little eyes go blink, blink, blink.
One little hand goes snap, snap, snap.
Two little hands go clap, clap, clap.
Now fold them quietly in your lap.

Head, Shoulders, Knees, and Toes
(This song may be done first in normal rhythm, then slow motion, then fast motion, to get lots of energy out.)

Head and shoulders, knees and toes,
Knees and toes.
Head and shoulders, knees and toes,
Knees and toes.
Eyes and ears and mouth and nose,
Head and shoulders, knees and toes,
Knees and toes.

De Cabeza a los Dedos

Cabeza, hombros, rodillas y dedos,
Rodillas y dedos.
Cabeza, hombros, rodillas y dedos,
Rodillas y dedos.
Ojos, orejas, boca, y nariz,
Cabeza, hombros, rodillas y dedos,
Rodillas y dedos.

Two Little Hands

(sung to the tune of "Ten Little Indians")
Two little hands, ten little fingers. [Hold up two fists, then show ten
    fingers.]
Two little hands, ten little fingers. Two little hands, ten little fingers.
Count them all with me.
One little, two little, three little fingers.
Four little, five little, six little fingers.
Seven little, eight little, nine little fingers.
We all have ten fingers.

Dos Manitas

(sung to the tune of "Ten Little Indians")
Dos manitas, diez deditos,
Dos manitas, diez deditos,
Dos manitas, diez deditos,
Cuéntenlos conmigo,
Uno, dos, tres deditos
Cuatro, cinco, seis deditos
Siete, ocho, nueve deditos
Diez deditos tengo.

In Spanish, the same tune can be sung using colors:
Rojo, verde, amarillo.
Blanco, negro, anaranjado,
Gris, café, azul, morado,
¡Diez colores tengo!

How Many Fingers?

Do you know? Do you know?
How many fingers I'm going to show?
(Show a number of fingers. Group counts and responds.)

Retintín

Retintín, retintón
¿Cuántos, cúantos dedos son?

Touch
Touch your shoulders,
Touch your knees,
Raise your arms,
Then drop them please.
Touch your ankles,
Then touch your toes,
Pull your ears,
Then touch your nose.
With your toes go
Tap, tap, tap.
Now your fingers
Snap, snap, snap.
Stretch as high as high can be.
While you're there,
Clap one, two, three.

Toca
Mis hombritos, mis rodillas,
Así extiendo mis bracitos,
Mis tobillos, y mis pies,
Mis oídos, enseño diez [fingers].
Con mis pies me paro así,
Y mis dedos trueno así.
Luego yo me estiro pues,
Y aplaudo uno, dos, tres.

Where Is Thumbkin?
Where is Thumbkin?
Where is Thumbkin?
Here I am.
Here I am.
How are you today, sir?
Very well I thank you.
Run away, run away.

Repeat, substituting for the first two lines:

Where is Pointer?
Where is Tall Finger?
Where is Ring Finger?
Where is Little Finger?
Where is everybody?

Mi Cuerpo y Yo
Yo me levanto, estoy de pie.
Cuento los dedos, uno, dos, tres.
Abro la boca, cierro los ojos.

Me toco los labios que son rosas.
Giro a la derecha, estoy contento,
Saco la lengua por un momento.
Abro los ojos, miro al cielo.
Me toco la cabeza, cubierto de pelo,
Doy palmadas, levanto el brazo.
Giro a la izquierda y doy un paso.

INCLUSION SONGS

These songs either use the children's own names or involve the group in making up new verses. In these ways, they help the children feel part of the class.

The More We Get Together
The more we get together, together, together,
The more we get together,
The happier you'll be.
There's [child's name] and [child's name] [continue to name children as
    they are ready, or as you want to excuse them to line].
The happier you'll be.

Cuanto Más Nos Juntemos
Cuanto más nos juntemos, nos juntemos, nos juntemos,
Cuanto más nos juntemos,
Más contento/a estoy.
Hay [child's name] y [child's name] [continue to name children as they are
    ready, or as you want to excuse them to line].
Más contento/a estoy.

If You're Happy and You Know It
If you're happy and you know it, clap your hands.
If you're happy and you know it, clap your hands.
If you're happy and you know it,
Then your face will surely show it.
If you're happy and you know it, clap your hands.
If you're happy and you know it, tap your foot.
If you're happy and you know it, tap your foot.
If you're happy and you know it,
Then your face will surely show it.
If you're happy and you know it, tap your foot.
(Ask the children to give other motions. Sing each.)

Cuando Tengas Muchas Ganas
(adaptación en español por Silvia Padilla)
Cuando tengas muchas ganas de aplaudir.

Cuando tengas muchas ganas de aplaudir.

Cuando tengas la ilusión y no hay intervención no te quedes con las ganas de aplaudir.

Cuando tengas muchas ganas de brincar.

Cunado tengas muchas ganas de brincar.

Cuando tengas la ilusión y no hay intervención no te quedes con las ganas de brincar.

(Change the verb for each new verse to do new actions or to practice letter sounds [e.g., cepillar—ch, ch; beber—g, g; comer—m, m])

An adaptation of If You're Happy and You Know It/Cuando Tengas Muchas Ganas *follows. Use this to develop phonemic awareness.*

If you think you know the word, tell me it. *(Clap, clap)*

If you think you know the word, tell me it. *(Clap, clap)*

If you think you know the word, if you think you know the word, if you think you know the word, tell me it. *(Clap, clap)* /d/ /o/ /g/

Si tu sabes la palabra, dímela. *(Clap, clap)*

Si tu sabes la palabra, dímela. *(Clap, clap)*

Si tu sabes la palabra, si tu sabes la palabra, si tu sabes la palabra, dímela. *(Clap, clap)* /r/ /a/ /n/ /a/

Cookie Jar

Group: Who stole the cookie from the cookie jar?

[Name of child] stole the cookie from the cookie jar.

Individual: Who me?

Group: Yes, you!

Individual: Couldn't be!

Group: Then who?

Individual: [Name of another child.]

(Group begins the chant again with that child's name and so on.)

Rhythm Chant

Start a snap, clap, slap knees rhythm. Have the children join with you. Then, on each snap, say a child's name. Go around the group, saying each child's name in turn. For example: clap, slap knees, José (snap while saying José); clap, slap knees, María; clap, slap knees, Wendy; and so on.

Sally Go Round the Sun

(As the group sings this song, one child skips around the outside of the circle [substitute that child's name for "Sally" after the children have learned the song]. On the words "Every afternoon," he or she taps another child to trade places. Repeat.)

Sally [or other child's name] go round the sun.

Sally go round the moon.

Sally go round the chimney pot

Every afternoon.

Johnny Works With One Hammer

Johnny [or any child's name] works with one hammer, one hammer, one
   hammer [pounding motion with one hand],
Johnny works with one hammer, then he works with two.
Johnny works with two hammers, two hammers, two hammers [pounding
   motion with both hands],
Johnny works with two hammers, then he works with three.
Johnny works with three hammers, three hammers, three hammers [add
   foot to pounding motions],
Johnny works with three hammers, then he works with four.
Johnny works with four hammers, four hammers, four hammers [jump up
   and down, still making pounding motions with hands],
Johnny works with four hammers, then he works with five.
Johnny works with five hammers, five hammers, five hammers [add head
   nodding to other motions],
Johnny works with five hammers, then he goes to sleep [lay head on
   hands].

Juanito Tiene un Martillo

Juanito tiene un martillo, un martillo, un martillo.
Juanito tiene un martillo, y luego tiene dos.
. . . con dos, tres, cuatro, y cinco, y luego se va a dormir.

SONGS THAT ARE ADAPTABLE TO THEMATIC UNITS

It is often difficult to find enough songs and poems specifically suited to
a particular topic. The following songs and chants can be adapted to fit any
thematic unit. Just make some simple stick puppets, and you have an instant
dramatization.

Five Little Monkeys (Bears, Elephants, Pumpkins)

Five little monkeys jumping on the bed.
One fell off and bumped his head.
Mommy called the doctor
And the doctor said,
"No more monkeys jumping on the bed!"
(Repeat, counting down verse by verse to one monkey.)

Cinco Monitos

Cinco monitos saltaron alegremente.
Uno se cayó y se pegó en la frente.
Mamá llamó al medicó y dijo fuertemente,
"¡Qué paren de brincar inmediatamente!"
Entonces . . . cuatro monitos, etc.

One Elephant (Bear, Car, Dinosaur) Went Out to Play

One elephant went out to play
On a spider's web one day.
He had such enormous fun,
He called for another elephant to come.
Two elephants went out to play.
On a spider's web one day.
They had such enormous fun,
They called for another elephant to come.
(Continue with three to ten elephants.)

Un Elefante (Oso, Carro, Dinosaurio) Se Balanceaba

Un elefante se balanceaba
Sobre la tela de una araña.
Como vela que resistía,
Fue a llamar a otro elefante.
Dos elefantes se balanceaban
Sobre la tela de una araña.
Como veía que resistían,
Fueron a llamar a otro elefante.
(Continue with tres *through* diez.*)*

Ten Little Brown Bears (Dinosaurs, Ants)

(sung to the tune of "Ten Little Indians")
One little, two little, three little brown bears,
Four little, five little, six little brown bears,
Seven little, eight little, nine little brown bears,
Ten little brown bears in a row.

Diez Ositos (Dinosaurios, Hormigas)

Uno, dos, tres ositos,
Cuatro, cinco, seis ositos.
Siete, ocho, nueve ositos.
Diez ositos chiquitos.

The Wheels on the Bus

The wheels on the bus go 'round and 'round, 'round and 'round, 'round and 'round.
The wheels on the bus go 'round and 'round,
All through the city streets
The people on the bus go up and down, up and down, up and down.
The people on the bus go up and down,
All through the city streets.
The wipers on the bus go swish, swish, swish; swish, swish, swish; swish, swish, swish.
The wipers on the bus go swish, swish, swish,
All through the city streets.

The baby on the bus goes wah, wah, wah, [and so on].
The money on the bus goes clink, clink, clink, [and so on].

Las Ruedas del Bus

Las ruedas del bus van ran, ran, ran; ran, ran, ran; ran, ran, ran.
Las ruedas del bus van ran, ran, ran por toda la ciudad.
La gente en el bus sube y baja, sube y baja, sube y baja.
La gente en el bus sube y baja por toda la ciudad.
Las monedas en el bus hacen clin, clin, clin; clin, clin, clin; clin, clin, clin, etc.
La bocina del bus va tu, tu ,tu; tu, tu, tu; tu, tu, tu, etc.
Los bebes en el bus hacen bua, bua, bua; bua, bua, bua; bua, bua, bua, etc.
Sus padres del bus hacen chi, chi, chi; chi, chi, chi; chi, chi, chi, etc.

Follow-Up Activity

1. This song lends itself to having the children create more verses, with accompanying noises and movements. Brainstorm other things that could happen on a bus and make up new verses.

2. Transfer the verses onto large pieces of construction paper—one verse per page. Have the children pair up, and then have each set of partners illustrate a verse. (You might want to provide the outline of a bus.) Bind all the pages together to make a class book.

3. Tape-record the children singing the song according to the class book. Place the book and the tape in the listening center for repeated listenings at free-choice time.

7

Home and School Communication

This chapter provides sample letters to communicate with parents and guardians in English and Spanish including letters about teacher expectations on the first day of school.

This chapter also includes requests for donations, opportunities for volunteering in the classroom as well as communications about homework and your writing program. These communications are meant be adapted to meet your classroom needs.

First Day of Kindergarten

Dear Parents and Guardians:

It's been hard to believe that summer is almost over, but here we are, about to embark on what I hope will be an exciting and productive year for your child. I am anxious to see that we have a smooth beginning. To ensure that, I am listing a few of the ways you can help _____ adjust to his or her first day of school.

1. To alleviate your child's first-day fears, talk to him or her about what to anticipate: that school will be a fun, busy learning time.

2. Arrive early (anytime after _____), to room _____, next _____, so that I can have an opportunity to greet you.

3. Once the first school bell rings, I will ask all parents and guardians to leave the room. This will make it easier for the children and me to bond and will facilitate your child's adaptation to school. I do want family members in the classroom later on, because I strongly believe that your involvement is key to your child's success. I will be making a strong plea for family volunteers in a few weeks.

4. If your child rides the bus home that first day, assure him or her that you will be waiting at the bus stop when he or she arrives. I will have a list of the bus stops posted in the classroom.

I am looking forward to meeting you!

Primer Día del Kinder

Estimados Padres y Guardianes:

Parece imposible que ya casi se terminó el verano, pero así es; y estamos a punto de embarcarnos en un nuevo año escolar. Espero que sea un año productivo y estimulante para su hijo o hija. Mi mayor deseo es que el principio de este año sea tranquilo. Para asegurarnos de que _____ se adapte fácilmente en su primer día de escuela, les sugierio lo siguiente:

1. Para reducir la ansiedad del primer día de escuela, hable con él o ella sobre lo que pueda anticipar: Que ir a la escuela es divertido y que van a estar muy ocupados aprendiendo muchas cosas nuevas.

2. Llegue temprano (despues de las _____), al aula _____ el próximo _____, para que yo pueda tener la oportunidad de darles la bienvenida.

3. En cuanto suene la campana, les voy a pedir a todos los padres que se retiren del aula para que se puede establecer el vinculo entre los niños y la maestra. Así será más fácil que los niños se acostumbren a la escuela. Más adelante voy a querer la presencia de los padres en el aula porque creo que la clave del éxito escolar se halla en su participación. En unas semanas voy a pedirles a los padres que sirvan como voluntarios en el aula.

4. Si su hijo se va a casa en el autobus el primer día, asegúreles que ustedes van a estar esperandolo en la parada cuando llegue. Tendré una lista de las paradas del autobus en el aula.

¡Espero el gusto de conocerlos!

Donation Requests

Dear Parents and Guardians:

Donation List

We are in need of some materials for our art center. If you have any of these items to donate, we would greatly appreciate it.

Fabric scraps
Paper towel rolls
Colored pencils
Buttons
Shells
Seeds, beans, peas
Yarn
String
Ribbon
Different shapes of macaroni
Popsicle sticks
Needles and thread
Felt pieces
Small wood scraps
Squares of cardboard
Felt-tip markers (fat and thin)
Toothpicks
Straws
Bottle caps
Spools
Measuring cups and spoons
Sponges (old)
Old shirts

Donaciones, Por Favor

Estimados Padres y Guardianes:

Lista de Donativo

Necesitamos algunos materiales para el centro del arte. Si ustedes tienen algunos de estos materiales disponibles para donarnos, se lo agradeceremos mucho.

Pedazos de tela
Rollos de papel de cocina
Lápices de color
Botones
Conchas del mar
Semillas, frijoles, chicharos
Hilo de lana
Cordón
Listón
Diversas formas de macarrones
Palitos de paletas
Hilos y agujas
Tela de fieltro
Pedazos de madera chicos
Cuadros de cartón
Rotuladores (gordos y delgados)
Palillos
Popotes
Corcholatas de botella
Carretes de hilo vacíos
Tazas y cucharas para medir
Esponjas (viejas)
Camisas viejas

Daily Snack Program

Dear Parents and Guardians:

Our class has voted to have a daily snack at approximately _____. It was decided that each child who wanted to participate would bring a healthy snack about once a month. I will send home a note announcing your child's day to bring a snack. Some suggestions are crackers, cheese, fruit, baked goods, nuts, raisins, granola, popcorn, carrots, celery, or other vegetables. There are generally _____ people in the classroom.

Your support in this program is appreciated. If you would prefer that your child not participate, just send a note or call. If you have any other questions or concerns, feel free to get in touch.

Thank you,

Your child is scheduled to bring a snack on _____.

Programa Diario Del Bocadillo

Estimados Padres y Guardianes:

Nuestra clase ha votado a favor de tener un bocadillo a las _____ aproximadamente. Se decidió que cada niño que quiera participar traiga un bocadillo nutritivo una vez al mes. Voy a mandar un recado indicándoles el día que le va a tocar a su hijo o hija traer algo. Algunos de los bocadillos que sugerimos son galletas, queso, fruta, postres elaborados en casa, frutos secos, pasas, granola, palomitas de maíz, zanahorias, apio, o alguna otra verdura. Por lo general hay _____ personas en la clase.

Su apoyo en este programa será muy agradecido. Si prefieren que su hijo o hija no participe en este programa, nada más manden una nota o comuníquemelo por teléfono. Si tienen ustedes alguna pregunta o algo les preocupe comuníquemelo con confianza.

Gracias,

El día que le toca a su hijo o hija traer bocadillo es _____.

Classroom Volunteer Request

Dear Parents and Guardians:

I realize you are busy with your jobs, lives, and families. If time permits, I'd love your help in the classroom. Please take a few minutes to look over the following list to see if you can help.

[ ] Typing. Commitment: twice during the year.
[ ] Handle book club orders. Commitment: once a month or every six to ten weeks.
[ ] Working with individuals or a small group with math. Commitment: once a month to several times a week.
[ ] Listening to children read aloud, any day except Friday. Commitment: once a month to several times a week.
[ ] Leading a literature group (leading a discussion of a novel with a small group of children), any day except Friday, 8:45–9:40. Commitment: once or twice a week for the duration of the book.
[ ] Room parent (general support and primarily help with the carnival— the children pretty well organize their own parties).
[ ] Talking to the class or small group about your career. Commitment: one time, to be arranged after December.
[ ] Driving on field trips (you must have insurance and seat belts).
[ ] Cooking with small groups of students.
[ ] Reading to the class once a week, Monday–Thursday, 1:00–1:30.
[ ] Anything I missed?

If you have any questions or need more information before signing your time away, please call me at _____

Thank you,

_____

Parent/Guardian's name   Parent/Guardian's telephone number

_____

Parent/Guardian's e-mail address

Voluntarios, Por Favor

Estimados Padres y Guardianes:

Comprendo que están muy ocupados con su trabajo, su vida, y demás responsabilidades en casa. Si tienen el tiempo, me encantaría contar con su ayuda en mi aula. Por favor tomen un momento para revisar la lista abajo para ver si pueden ayudarme.

[ ] Escribir en máquina. Obligación: solamente dos veces al año.

[ ] Hacerse cargo de hacer los pedidos del Libro del Mes. Obligación: una vez al mes o cada seis a diez semanas.

[ ] Dirigir un grupo de literatura (dirigir una discusión de una novela con un grupo de niños), cualquier día excepto los viernes, 8:45–9:40. Obligación: una o dos veces a la semana o hasta que se termine el libro.

[ ] Madre o padre del aula (apoyo general, principalmente con el carnaval— los estudiantes más o menos organizan sus fiestas en la clase por sí mismos.

[ ] Visitar el aula y hablar acerca de su ocupación. Obligación: una vez nada más, y concretaremos las fechas después de diciembre.

[ ] Ayudar a transportar a los estudiantes en las excursiones escolares (se debe poseer un seguro de carro y cinturones de seguridad).

[ ] Cocinar con un grupo pequeño de estudiantes.

[ ] Leer a la clase en voz alta una vez por semana, lunes a jueves, 1:00–1:30.

[ ] Algo más que se me olvidó mencionar?

Si tienen alguna pregunta o necesitan información adicional antes de comprometer su tiempo, por favor llame al _____.

Gracias,

_____   _____
Nombre de padre o guardián   Teléfono de padre o guardián

_____
Email address de los padres/de los guardas

Homework Schedule

Dear Parents and Guardians:

This is a note about homework. Your child will have homework every night except Fridays. The intent of the homework is threefold: (a) it helps to build responsibility in the children, as they are responsible for the completion and the transportation of the work; (b) it gives the students an opportunity to practice skills taught in the class; and (c) it gives you a chance to become involved with your child's class work.

Children are most successful with homework if the time and place for work are consistent. A quiet desk to work at and a regular time, such as right before or after dinner, seem to be the most beneficial.

A copy of your student's homework schedule follows. Please keep it as a reminder.

Thank you,

Homework Schedule

Monday:

Tuesday:

Wednesday:

Thursday:

Horario de la Tarea

Estimados Padres y Guardianes:

Les envío esta nota en referencia a la tarea. Su hijo o hija tendrá tarea todos los días excepto el viernes. La tarea sirve tres propósitos: (a) ayuda al estudiante a ser responsable de hacer el trabajo, completarlo y transportarlo; (b) le da al estudiante la oportunidad de practicar la habilidades adquiridas en la clase; y (c) les da a ustedes la oportunidad de envolucrarseen el trabajo escolar de su estudiante.

Los estudiantes tienen más éxito cuando el lugar y la hora de hacer la tarea es siempre lo mismo. Escoja un lugar determinado y cómodo para que su hijo o hija haga su tarea, guarde sus papeles y recuerde traer la tarea a clase al día siguiente.

Abajo está el programa diario de tarea. Por favor guárdelo como un recordatorio.

Gracias,

Programa Diario de la Tarea

Lunes:

Martes:

Miércoles:

Jueves:

The Writing Process

Dear Parents and Guardians:

This year we are working on the writing process. This process involves these main steps:

1. Prewriting: thinking, getting started

2. Rough drafts: writing ideas down

3. Revising: making the words clearer, the content more interesting; making additions, deletions, changes

4. Editing and proofreading: correcting spelling, grammar, punctuation

5. Publishing: completing the finished work, final copy

Not all writing will go through all five steps. Some may go through only Step 2 or 3. In that case, a paper that comes home would be stamped "unedited," which means it was checked for content only.

If your child asks you to read a piece of his or her writing, ask if you are reading it (a) for enjoyment (sharing), (b) for comments about the content (Is it understandable?), or (c) for editing (correcting spelling, punctuation, grammar). Your responses would vary according to the purpose. Here are some suggested comments or questions:

1. Enjoyment: Wonderful! I really liked this part . . . How did you think of this idea?

2. Content: I'm not sure what you mean here. This part is not very clear. Read it out loud to me. It doesn't feel finished—are you going to write more?

3. Editing: Is it okay if I write on your paper? Should I use a pen or pencil?

It is my hope that this will help you and your child enjoy writing and the written word together.

Sincerely,

El Proceso De la Escritura

Estimados Padres y Guardianes:

Estamos trabajando en el proceso de la escritura este año. Este proceso consiste en los siguientes pasos principales:

1. Antes de escribir: pensar, prepararse para empezar

2. Escribir: escribir ideas en papel

3. Revisar: hacer más claras las palabras, hacer más interesante el contenido; agregar, tachar, hacer cambios

4. Repaso y corrección de pruebas: corregir ortografía, gramática, y puntuación

5. Publicación: terminar el trabajo completo, copiar en limpio

No todos los trabajos de escritura van a seguir los cinco pasos. Algunos trabajos nada más van a seguir pasos dos o tres. En ese caso los trabajos que los alumnos lleven a casa tendrán un sello que ponga "no corregido," lo cual quiere decir que solamente el contenido ha sido revisado, no la ortografía, gramática ni la puntuación.

Si su hijo o hija le pide a usted que lean algo que ellos han escrito, pregúntele para qué propósito: (a) por el gusto de compartir, (b) para comentarios sobre el contenido (¿Se entiende?), o (c) para hacer correcciones de ortografía, puntuación, y gramática. Sus respuestas van a variar según el propósito de la pregunta. Los siguientes comentarios o preguntas son recomendables.

1. Por el gusto de compartir: Magnífico, de veras me gusta esta parte . . . ¿Cómo se te ocurrió esa idea?

2. Contenido: No estoy muy seguro/a de lo que quieres decir aquí. Esta parte no está muy clara. Lee esta parte en voz alta. Parece que el idea no está completa—¿vas a escribir más?

3. Correcciones: ¿Puedo escribir en tu papel? ¿Prefieres que utilice pluma o lápiz?

Es mi esperanza que este ejercicio les ayude a ustedes y a su hijo o hija disfruten de la escritura y la palabra escrita.

Sinceramente,

Resource A: Bibliography for Teachers

The books in the following bibliography are good sources of activities as are those mentioned in the previous chapters.

Conflict Resolution

Kreidler, W. J. (1984). *Creative conflict resolution: More than 200 ideas for keeping peace in the classroom.* Santa Monica, CA: Goodyear.

Literacy

Atwell, N. (1987). *In the middle: Writing, reading, and learning with adolescents.* Portsmouth, NH: Heinemann.

Bear, D., Invernizzi, M. A., & Templeton, S. (2007). *Words their way.* Upper Saddle River, NJ: Prentice-Hall.

Bishop, A. S. (2004). *Teaching phonics, phonemic awareness, and word recognition.* Westminster, CA: Teacher Created Materials.

Calkins, L. M., & McEnvoy, M. (2006) *Units of Study for Teaching Writing.* Portsmouth, NH: Heinemann.

Cunningham, P., & Allington, R. (2006). *Classrooms that work: They can all read and write.* New York: HarperCollins.

Cunningham, P., & Hall, D. (2001). *Making words.* Carthage, IL: Good Apple.

Fontas, I., & Pinnell, G. S. (1996). *Guided reading: Good first teaching for all children.* Portsmouth, NH: Heinemann.

Routman, R. (2000). *Reading Essentials: The Specifics You Need to Teach Reading Well.* Portsmouth, NH: Heinemann.

Tinajero, J., & Schifini, A. (1996). *Into English! Teachers' guide for any level.* Carmel, CA: Hampton Brown.

Math

Baratta-Lorton, M. (1976). *Mathematics Their Way.* Menlo Park, CA: Addison-Wesley.

Baratta-Lorton, R. (1977). *Mathematics: A Way of Thinking.* Menlo Park, CA: Addison-Wesley.

Burns, M. (1987). *A Collection of Math Lessons from Grades 1 through 3.* New Rochelle, NY: Cuisenaire.

Burns, M. (1987). *A Collection of Math Lessons from Grades 3 through 6.* New Rochelle, NY: Cuisenaire.

Bums, M. (n.d.). *The Good Time Math Event Book.* Concord, CA: Creative Publications.

Carpenter, T., Franke, M., & Levi, L. (2003) *Thinking Mathematically: Integrating Arithmetic & Algebra in Elementary School.* Portsmouth, NH: Heinemann.

Carpenter, T., Fennema, E., Franke, M., Levi, L., & Empson, S. (1999) *Children's Mathematics: Cognitively Guided Instruction.* Portsmouth, NH: Heinemann.

Chapin, S. H., & Johnson, A. (2006) *Math Matters: Understanding the Math You Teach.* Sausalito, CA: Math Solutions Publication.

Cossey, R., Stenmark, J. K., & Thompson, V. (1986). *Family Math.* Berkeley: Lawrence Hall of Science/University of California Regents.

Physical Education

Fluegelman, A. (1976). *The New Games Book.* Garden City, NY: Dolphin/Doubleday.

Harris, F. (1990). *Games.* Belmont, CA: Fearon Teacher Aids/Simon & Schuster.

Kamiya, A. (1985). *Elementary Teacher's Handbook of Indoor & Outdoor Games.* Englewood Cliffs, NJ: Prentice Hall.

Tames, C. (1983). *Awesome Elementary School Physical Education Activities.* (Available from the author at 3949 Linus Way, Carmichael, California).

Team Building, Self-Esteem

Gibbs, J. (2006). *Reaching All by Creating Tribes Learning Communities.* Berkeley, CA: Center Source.

Howe, L., Kershenbaum, H., & Simon, S. B. (1997). *Values Clarification.* Denver, CO: Hart.

Kagan, S. (1997). *Cooperative Learning.* San Juan Capistrano, CA: Resources for Teachers.

White, E. (1980). *Nourishing the Seeds of Self-Esteem.* Capitola, CA: Whitenwife.

Web Sites

Math Solutions Professional Development. http://www.mathsolutions.com (Math lessons for grades K–5).

TeacherWeb. http://www.teacherweb.com (Create a web page).

Create a Rubric. http://www.rubistar.com (Make your own rubric).

Resource B:
Read-Alouds,
K–6, in English
and Spanish

English

Book titles in this list that are followed by asterisks are also available in Spanish.

Kindergarten

Benjamin's 365 Birthdays, Judi Barrett (Illustrated by Ron Barrett. 2nd Aladdin Books ed. New York: Maxwell Macmillan International, 1992; Atheneum, 1974; pa. Simon & Schuster, 1992)

Caps for Sale, Esphyr Slobodkira (Scholastic Book Services, 1966)

Corduroy,* Don Freeman (HarperCollins, 1947)

Goodnight Moon, Margaret Wise Brown (Illustrated by Clement Hurd. HarperTrophy, 1977)

Ira Sleeps Over, Bernard Waber (A Walter Lorraine Book, Houghton Mifflin Company, 1975)

Rosie's Walk, Pat Hutchins (Aladdin, 1968)

The Snowy Day, Ezra Jack Keats (Viking Juvenile, 1962)

First Grade

The Carrot Seed, Ruth Krauss (Illustrated by Crockett Johnson. Gryphon House, Inc. 1945)

Curious George,* H. A. Rey (Houghton Mifflin, 1941)

Noisy Nora, Rosemary Wells (Puffin Books, 1973)

Rhymes About Us, Marchette Chute (Dutton Books, 1974)

Stone Soup, Marcia Brown (Charles Scribners Sons, New York, 1947)

Tikki, Tikki Tembo, Arlene Mosel (Henry Holt and Co., 1968)

Second Grade

A Birthday for Frances, Russell Hoban (Scholastic, 1968)

The Carp in the Bathtub, Barbara Cohen (Illustrated by Joan Halpern. Kar-Ben Publishing, Inc., 1972)

Family Pictures, Carmen Lomas Garza (Children's Book Press, 1990)

Frog and Toad Are Friends, Arnold Lobel (HarperCollins, 1970)

The Island of the Skog, Steven Kellogg (Puffin Books, 1993)

Miss Nelson Is Missing, Harry Allard (Houghton Mifflin Company, New York, 1977)

Stone Soup, Marcia Brown (Charles Scribners Sons, New York, 1947)

Sylvester and the Magic Pebble, William Steig (Windmill Books, Inc., 1907)

Third Grade

A Bear Called Paddington, Michael Bond (Houghton Mifflin, New York, 1958, 1986)

The Borrowers, Mary Norton (Odyssey/Harcourt Young, 1953)

Charlotte's Web, E. B. White (HarperCollins Publishers Inc., 1952)

The Great Brain, John Fitzgerald (Yearling, New York, 1972)

The Lion, the Witch, and the Wardrobe, C. S. Lewis (Illustrated by Pauline Baynes. Geoffrey Bles, 1950.)

Miss Rumphius, Barbara Cooney (Viking Penguin Inc., 1982)

The Mouse and the Motorcycle, Beverly Cleary (HarperCollins Publishers Inc., 1965)

Soup on Fire, Robert Newton Peck (Delacorte Books for Young Readers, 1987)

Strega Nona, Tomi DePaola (Simon & Schuster, New York, 1975)

Stuart Little, E. B. White (HarperCollins Publishers Inc., 1945)

Fourth Grade

From the Mixed-Up Files of Mrs. Basil E. Frankweiler, E. L. Koningsburg (Bantam Doubleday Dell Publishing Group, Inc., New York, 1967)

The Girl Who Cried Flowers, Jane Yolen (Illustrated by David Palladini. T. Y. Crowell, 1974)

House on Mango Street, Sandra Cisneros (Arte Publico Press, 1984)

Island of the Blue Dolphins, Scott O'Dell (Random House, Inc., New York, 1960)

James and the Giant Peach, Roald Dahl (Alfred A. Knopf, Inc., 1961)

Mrs. Frisby and the Rats of NIMH, Robert C. O'Brien (Aladdin Paperbacks, 1975)

Ramona the Pest, Beverly Cleary (William Morrow and Company, Inc., 1968)

Tales of a Fourth Grade Nothing, Judy Blume (Bantam Doubleday Dell Publishing Group, Inc., New York, 1972)

Fifth Grade

The Incredible Journey, Sheila Burnford (Bantam Doubleday Dell Publishing Group, Inc., New York, 1960)

Owls in the Family, Farley Mowat (Bantam Doubleday Dell Publishing Group, Inc., New York, 1961)

Philip Hall Likes Me, I Reckon . . . Maybe, Bette Greene (Penguin Group, New York, 1974)

The Pinballs, Betsy Byars (HarperCollins Publishers Inc., New York, 1977)

The Sign of the Beaver, Elizabeth Speare (Bantam Doubleday Dell Publishing

Group, Inc., New York, 1983)
Sing Down the Moon, Scott O'Dell (Random House, Inc., New York, 1970)
Summer of the Swans, Betsy Byars (Penguin Putnam Inc., New York, 1970)

Sixth Grade

Bridge to Terabithia,* Katherine Paterson (HarperCollins Publishers Inc., New York, 1977)
Call It Courage, Armstrong Sperry (Collier Books, 1971)
Ring of Endless Light, Madeleine L'Engle (Random House, Inc., New York, 1976)
Roll of Thunder, Hear My Cry, Mildred D. Taylor (Dial Books, 1976)
Sounder, William H. Armstrong (HarperCollins Publishing Inc., 1969)

Spanish

Kindergarten

A la cama monstruito!, Mario Ramos, Corimbo, 2001
Abuela cuentamos un cuento, Rocio Martinez, Grupo Anaya, 2002
Adonde va el agua?, Jeanne Ashbe, Corimbo, 2000
Corduroy, Don Freeman
Donde viven los monstruos, Maurice Sendak
La historia de la pollita, Mary DeBall Kwitz
El oso más elegante, Mary Blocksman
El primer día de escuela, Helen Oxenbury
Tortillitas para Mamá, Griego y Bucks

First Grade

Angus y el gato, Marjorie Flack
El arbol generoso, Shel Silverstein, Litexsa Venezolana, 1999
Corduroy, Don Freeman, Penguin, 1990
¿Eres tú mi Mama?, P. D. Eastman
Jorge el Curioso, H. A. Rey
Nadarín, Leo Lionni
El poni, el oso y el manzano, Sigrid Heuck

Second Grade

Buenos días, querida ballena, Achim Broger
Osito, Else H. Minarik
Sapo y Sepo, inseparables, Arnold Lobel
Sylvestre y la piedra mágica, William Steig
El vejo reloj, Fernando Alonso
Willy el timido, Anthony Browne, Fondo de Cultura Economica, 1991
Yo, el gran fercho y el ladron, Majorie Weinman Sharmat , Grupo Editorial Norma, 1995

Third Grade

Las aventuras de connie y diego, Carolyn García
Crisantemo, Kevin Henkes, Everest, 1993
Cuando los cuervos eran multicolores, Edith Schreiber-Wicke and Carola
    Holland, Juventud, 1995
Cuantos es un million?, David M. Schwartz, Scholastic,1993
Gracias, tejon, Susan Varley, Santillanna, 1985
Hansel y Gretel, los Hermanos Grimm
El patito feo, Hans Christian Andersen
Ramona la chinche, Beverly Cleary

Fourth Grade

La ballena, Judy Blume, Bradbury Press, 1983
Las bellas hijas de Mufaro, John Steptoe, Lothrop, Lee & Shephard Books,
    1997
La bruja que quiso matar al sol, Ricardo Alcántara
Un caballo llamado Libertad, Pam Munoz Ryan , Scholastic, 2001
La calle es libre, Kurusa
Platero y Yo, Juan Ramón Jiménez
Las telarañas de carlota, E. B. White

Fifth Grade

El autobus magico en el cuerpo humano, Joanna Cole, Scholastic, 1993
La isla de los delfines azules, Scott O'Dell, Caralt, 1996
El Mago de Oz, L. Frank Baum (Conaculta, 1991)
Petrosinella, Basile Giambattista y Diane Stanley

Sixth Grade

James y el melocotón gigante, Roald Dahl
Julie y los lobos, Jean Craighead George
El Principito, Antoine de Saint-Exupéry
Puente hasta Terabithia, Katherine Paterson
Rosie's Walk, Pat Hutchins
The Snowy Day, Ezra Jack Keats

CORWIN PRESS

The Corwin Press logo—a raven striding across an open book—represents the union of courage and learning. Corwin Press is committed to improving education for all learners by publishing books and other professional development resources for those serving the field of PreK–12 education. By providing practical, hands-on materials, Corwin Press continues to carry out the promise of its motto: **"Helping Educators Do Their Work Better."**